I0559214

⧸⧸⧸ AUTHORSUNITE

Copyright © 2025 by John P. Rosales

This playbook was written to inspire, challenge, and spark curiosity. It is not medical, nutritional, or mental health advice. I may talk about mindset, journaling, movement, and food, but I am not your doctor, therapist, or personal trainer. I am just an outsider sharing what I have observed and lived through on this planet.

If you are struggling with serious health, mental health, or medical concerns, please seek the help of a qualified Earthling professional. *Use this book as a guide for ideas, not prescriptions.*

Remember, every choice you make on this planet is yours. The power and the responsibility belong to you.

Edited by: Taylor Plimpton
Cover and Interior Design by Kurt A. Dierking II
Published by Authors Unite Publishing

ISBN: 978-1-960346-72-8

THE EARTHLING'S PLAYBOOK

A Practical Guide for Success on Planet Earth

STOIC ROCKSTAR

AUTHORSUNITE

TABLE OF CONTENTS

INTRODUCTION   1

1. YOU ARE...   5
2. JOURNALING   11
3. MEDITATION   25
4. HABITS   31
5. ENVIRONMENT   41
6. AFFIRMATIONS   47
7. MOVEMENT   53
8. FOOD   59
9. READERS ARE LEADERS   69
10. SLEEP   77
11. SUNRISE RITUALS   85
12. THE ART OF SHOWING UP   91
13. THE POWER OF CONSISTENCY   99
14. PURPOSE DRIVEN BEINGS   107
15. MAKE LIFE A GAME   115
16. UNCOMFORTABLY COMFORTABLE   125
17. CLOSED MOUTHS DON'T GET FED   129
18. IN ORDER TO RECEIVE, YOU MUST GIVE   137
19. MEDIA DEPRIVATION   143
20. UNDERSTANDING MENTAL ILLNESS   149
21. WE ARE...   155
22. BE GOOD TO FUTURE YOU   159

CONCLUSION   167

INTRODUCTION

Welcome to Earth, fellow stranger! If you feel like you've been dropped onto this planet out of nowhere and are expected to survive, I understand. 33 years ago, I landed in a small town in South Texas, where I faced firsthand the challenges of poverty, crime, negativity, and toxic habits. Every day was a battle for status, with the choice to fit in, stand out, or numb oneself. So rest assured, you are not alone! There is hope and opportunity for an incredible future for all of us—no matter where we land.

Do you realize how fortunate you are? Today, you have the chance to start with a clean slate and choose which behaviors, habits, and characteristics you want to adopt! (Actually, Earthlings have this option too, but many don't even realize it.) Through my own experiences, I've learned that it's possible to rise above anything and flourish in any environment. That's the purpose of this book—to equip you with the tools and guidance you need to thrive not only on this planet but anywhere, anytime. While some Earthlings may be content to follow the conventional 9-5 routine and chase after traditional markers of 'success'—like marriage, children, and retirement—we will focus on an unconventional approach, drawing from the fundamentals and traits observed in the most successful Earthlings.

It's crucial to recognize that your environment plays a significant role in shaping your destiny. However, with a simple shift in your mindset, thinking, and actions, you can overcome any obstacle and craft a life that aligns with your true aspirations.

EARTHLING TERMS
MADE SIMPLE
MINDSET

: A mindset is like a set of thoughts or beliefs that you have in your head. It can be positive or negative and it can affect how you feel and what you do. For example, if you have a positive mindset, you might believe that you can do hard things and that you are strong and brave. You might also see challenges as something fun to try and as a result you might try your best even when things are tough. On the other hand, if you have a negative mindset, you might believe that you can't do hard things and that you aren't very good at things in general. You might see challenges as something scary and you might not try your best because you think you'll fail anyways. A mindset is just a way of thinking, and you can choose to have a positive or negative mindset about anything.

Arriving here on Earth provides a blank canvas—a chance to paint a new beginning regardless of your past. As newcomers, you have the unique opportunity to shed old habits and foster new ones more aligned with the life you want to create. Similarly, Earthlings are afforded this chance each day, though they often overlook the power it holds. Every day, you wake up with the ability to make choices that shape your future. Whether it's the food you eat, the people you surround yourself with, or the thoughts you entertain, each decision steers your life's direction. This book isn't about lofty promises of immediate transformation but about recognizing the small, consistent actions that lead to meaningful change.

My journey into this lifestyle began out of necessity. Growing up in challenging circumstances, I realized that waiting for perfect conditions would lead to decades going by with no progress. Instead, I started focusing on what I could control—my habits, my mindset, and my actions. This shift didn't happen overnight, but with time and persistence, it led to profound changes. Writing this book was driven by my desire to share what I've learned in a way that is straightforward and relatable. I was blessed to be able to spend months and even years producing podcasts and content for some big names in the self-development world and I noticed that even though they would repeat the same things over and over, I still didn't understand what they were talking about. It's like they learned an extremely complicated secret but couldn't figure out a way to explain it simply to anyone else. If I couldn't understand it, then there's no way the average Earthling could, so that's where I stepped in.

I made it a personal challenge to break down the fundamentals in a fun way that's easy to read, looks great, and clicks with the outsiders who don't connect with the self-development world. There are thousands of self-help books out there, often filled with regurgitated information that can be confusing. My goal is to cut through the noise and provide clear, actionable steps that anyone can follow.

This book is a guide to help you navigate life on Earth with a fresh perspective. It's about adopting a mindset that sees possibilities rather than limitations. It's about understanding that you have the power to influence your own life and the lives of those around you. As you read through the chapters, I encourage you to keep an open mind and be willing to step out of your comfort zone. Remember, the journey to self-improvement is ongoing, and the most important step is the one you take today.

Mindset is key.
So remember, if you believe
the world is a magical place,
magical things will happen.

CHAPTER 1: YOU ARE...

"You are the books you read, the films you watch, the music you listen to, the people you meet, the dreams you have, the conversations you engage in. You are what you take from these."
—Chuck Palahniuk

On your journey through Earth, you may have noticed that Earthlings often focus heavily on their outward appearance. However, the true essence of who they are lies much deeper. Here's a saying you might find interesting: "You are what you eat." While this is often taken literally, implying that eating unhealthy foods can lead to poor health, there's a broader and more profound perspective to consider. What if I told you that you are also what you listen to, who you surround yourself with, and what you think? These elements play a crucial role in shaping who you become.

YOU ARE ...
WHAT YOU LISTEN TO

The first time I encountered the "You Are" concept was when I aspired to be a great musician. I was obsessed with seeking out the best players in town to pick their brains, and I discovered that many of them were jazz musicians. During a break, I approached the bass player and complimented his playing. When I asked him how he became so skilled, he told me that jazz was his life—he played it constantly, listened to it all the time, and didn't really have to try anymore. He then asked me what I listened to, and I responded with a cocky response like "Santana, Hendrix, Sabbath, The Beatles, Deep Purple, you know, the greats." He chuckled and replied, "You are what you listen to."

In that moment, I realized the truth of his words. If I wanted to be a proficient jazz player, I needed to immerse myself in the genre. However, I admitted to him that while I respected jazz as an art form and enjoyed seeing it live, I did not particularly enjoy listening to it. So, I decided to focus on mastering the music that truly moved me instead.

To become proficient at anything, consistency is key. This is especially true for jazz music—if you do not regularly listen to and practice jazz, it will be difficult to become a skilled jazz player. The same principles apply to other pursuits as well. You cannot expect to be a great writer if you don't read great books and practice writing every day. You cannot be a great athlete if you spend your waking hours on the couch. In order to succeed in any field, it's important to be consistent in your efforts and dedicate yourself to learning and improving.

YOU ARE ...
WHO YOU SURROUND YOURSELF WITH.

It's easy for wealthy Earthlings to generate wealth because everyone around them is good at making money. For many people living in poverty, the concept of making money can be foreign and intimidating. It may also feel like learning a new language, something that seems out of reach or impossible to achieve. For me, the only path to financial success was a college education or certification in a high-paying job—doing something that sucks away the soul and all your free time just to cover the basic necessities—but there was was never any talk in our community on how to properly manage money or invest it.

However, it's important to remember that every Earthling has the same same innate potential. While it may be easier for those with more privilege to get a head start, anyone can learn the skills and knowledge needed to be successful. As a wise Earthling said, "If you are born poor, it is not your mistake, but if you die poor, it is your mistake." This isn't just some rich Earthling's ego talking; it means that it's up to each individual to take advantage of the resources available and work towards financial success, even if it takes longer or requires more effort. Remember, the journey and the lessons learned along the way are ultimately the reward. Surround yourself with good people and your journey will be a smooth ride.

YOU ARE ...
WHAT YOU THINK.

If you believe that you are poor, then you will stay poor. If you see yourself as worthless and unattractive, that's what you'll become. The most important part of your journey on this planet is your mindset. If fear, anger, or overwhelm dominate your thoughts, those emotions will reflect back at you.

Regardless of setbacks, never lose faith in yourself. Keep pushing forward and never doubt your abilities. If you want it bad enough, you will achieve it. Too many Earthlings overestimate what they can accomplish in a year and underestimate what they can do in a decade. It's essential to set a realistic pace for yourself to ensure consistent growth year after year. The most successful individuals on this planet reached their pinnacle because they began and persisted. While most people never even start, maintaining a steady pace and continuous progress will propel you light-years ahead of the rest. And if you never give up, you'll surpass all those who quit along the way.

So, set attainable goals, because the funny thing about your goals is this...

DREAMS BECOME REALITY WHEN
YOU WRITE THEM DOWN AND PURSUE
THEM WITH DAILY ACTIONS.
DREAM BIG BECAUSE MOST PEOPLE
DON'T EVEN DO THAT.

CHALLENGE #1: OBSERVE YOUR INPUTS

This challenge is designed to help you become more aware of the influences shaping your life—what you listen to, who you surround yourself with, and what you think. For now, the goal is simply to observe. No action is required yet; just notice.

Step 1: Tune Into Your Environment

What You Listen To:

For one day, pay close attention to the media you consume—music, podcasts, news, TV shows, or even conversations. Notice how each one makes you feel. Does it energize you, inspire you, or bring you joy? Or does it leave you feeling drained, anxious, or distracted? At the end of the day, jot down a few notes about what you observed.

Who You Surround Yourself With:

Over the next few days, observe the people you spend time with. Notice how you feel during and after your interactions. Do you feel uplifted, supported, and inspired? Or do you feel drained, judged, or discouraged? Write down a few thoughts about what you notice.

What You Think:

Spend a few minutes each day simply observing your thoughts. Don't try to change them—just notice. Are your thoughts mostly positive, negative, or neutral? Are they focused on the past, present, or future? Write down a few observations about your mental patterns.

Step 2: Reflect

At the end of the week, take 10 minutes to reflect on what you've observed. Ask yourself: What patterns did I notice in my inputs? Are these inputs helping me become the person I want to be, or are they holding me back? What's one small change I might want to make in the future?

Why This Matters

The first step to growth is awareness. By observing your inputs—what you listen to, who you surround yourself with, and what you think—you'll gain valuable insights into the forces shaping your life. This awareness will prepare you for the deeper work of journaling, meditation, and affirmations that we'll explore in the coming chapters.

Take these challenges seriously and commit to doing the work. Real change happens when you step out of your comfort zone and take action. The more effort you invest, the greater the transformation you'll experience.

CHAPTER 2: JOURNALING

"Unexpressed emotions will never die."
—Sigmund Freud

One of the most significant breakthroughs I experienced during my time on this planet was learning how to clear space in my head. Did you know that your brain has limited capacity, much like a computer hard drive or phone storage? Every day, as you look at photos, watch videos, and engage in conversations, your subconscious saves these experiences into your brain's storage. While it might seem like your brain has infinite space, I assure you it does not.

Have you ever had someone ask you to remember something important before you leave? You confidently respond, "Of course, I'll remember," only to forget minutes later, letting them down. Or have you ever had a dream where you wrote the most wonderful song in the world, and you wake up for a brief moment at 3 a.m., thinking, "I'll just wait until morning to work on it"? But then, when you wake up, it's completely gone— no memory of the melody or anything. This could have been avoided if you had simply written down your thoughts. By holding onto unnecessary thoughts in your mind, you leave no room for the important ones. Do you really need to dwell on your dislike for work? You already know it, so jot it down! Do you need to constantly think about how unhappy you are with your current financial struggles? No, you don't. Write it down so you can free your mind from carrying it all day. That's the power of journaling.

When you journal, you liberate space in your mind. Your subconscious doesn't differentiate between your thoughts; if you dwell on something frequently, it assumes it's a priority and keeps it at the forefront. As a result, new thoughts are pushed to the bottom of the list, precisely when you need them the most. So don't be a thought hoarder! **Keeping your thoughts in your head is a terrible play because it can cause overwhelming feelings of anxiety, stress, and depression.** When you cling to your thoughts without writing them down, it becomes frustratingly difficult to process and understand them. Writing down your thoughts helps provide clarity and perspective, giving you an outlet to express your emotions. Journaling reduces stress, as it provides an opportunity to reflect on your life and daily experiences. Additionally, it helps to improve your problem-solving skills and boost your productivity and creativity.

Journaling is so important! Letting it all out on paper will improve your sleep and help you start the day like a champ. Write your goals for tomorrow, what you're grateful for, negative thoughts, positive thoughts, random thoughts. Journaling is really helpful for people who want to be successful on this planet. Here are a few reasons why:

1. Journaling helps you consider your thoughts and feelings objectively. When you write down your thoughts and feelings, you can better understand what's going on inside your mind. Do you notice any reoccurring patterns? This can help you solve problems and make better decisions.

2. Journaling helps you set goals and make plans. When you write down what you want to do and how you want to do it, it can be easier to make a plan and stick to it.

Imagine being trapped in an elevator alone. Except you're not alone. All of your thoughts manifest into random humans that start to take up space in the elevator. These random humans are selfish and talk overbearingly loud, speaking over you and battling each other to constantly be the loudest in the room. They make fun of you, doubt you, and remind you of all the failures from your past. They never give you a chance to speak.

SOUND FAMILIAR?

Now imagine they double and 30+ voices are speaking at the same time inside this elevator.

WELL THAT'S YOUR BRAIN WITHOUT A JOURNAL.

That unfortunate elevator ride could be a lot more peaceful by throwing all those random thoughts into a journal first thing in the morning and right before bed.

3. Journaling helps you remember things. Sometimes it's hard to remember everything that happens to us. When you write things down in a journal, you can look back and remember what happened. Your brain then sends these reminders to your long term memory.

4. Journaling can be fun! It's a chance to express yourself and be creative. You can write anything you want in your journal, and there's no right or wrong way to do it.

Overall, journaling is a tool for people who want to be successful in life. It can help you think about your thoughts and feelings, set goals and make plans, and remember things. Plus, it's fun! There is a reason why every successful human on this planet uses a journal.

Here are a few examples of successful people who have spoken about the importance of journaling in their lives:

Dwayne "The Rock" Johnson: While known for his larger-than-life persona, Johnson has shared that he journals regularly to stay grounded and focused. He uses writing to set goals, reflect on his journey, and maintain gratitude. His down-to-earth attitude and openness about his struggles make him a relatable figure despite his superstar status.

Kobe Bryant: The late NBA legend was known for his "Mamba Mentality," and part of that included journaling. Kobe used writing to reflect on his games, set goals, and analyze his performance. He even encouraged his daughters to journal as a way to build self-awareness and discipline. His dedication to self-improvement makes him an enduring inspiration.

Albert Einstein: One of the most famous scientists of all time, Einstein was also a regular journaler. He believed that writing down his thoughts and ideas helped him to better understand and organize them and improve his problem-solving skills.

Serena Williams: One of the greatest athletes of all time, Serena Williams has openly discussed how journaling helps her stay mentally focused and emotionally balanced. She uses her journal to reflect on her matches, set goals, and process the pressures of being a top athlete. Her discipline and vulnerability make her a relatable and inspiring figure for anyone striving to excel under pressure.

Frida Kahlo: The iconic Mexican artist used her journal as a space to explore her emotions, pain, and creativity. Filled with sketches, poems, and personal reflections, her journals offer a raw and intimate look into her inner world. Her journaling practice shows how writing can be a form of healing and self-expression.

These are just a few examples of successful people who have spoken about the importance of journaling in their lives. Many others have also credited journaling with helping them to achieve their goals and improve their lives.

CHALLENGE #2: THE MOST IMPORTANT JOURNALING EXERCISE

Let's do a journaling exercise right now. Set a timer for 10 minutes.

Now write about your end goal. Where do you see yourself in 10 years? What does your home look like? How do you wake up every morning? What kind of job do you have? What foods do you eat? What are you investing in? Get detailed and only focus on the vision of what your life looks like if you worked hard for 10 years straight and now have all the things you could imagine: a successful business, a vacation home on the beach, a black belt, a double platinum record. Reach for the stars! Timer starts..... Now.

Now that we know the end goal, let's reverse engineer this.

Set a timer for 10 more minutes, and write about: How did you receive this fortune? Was it from the business you started? How many people are working for you? Did you take a risk and invest in a great marketing team? Did you start a podcast along the road that helped push traffic to your website? Did you use an FHA loan to get your first house and now you leverage that house to live in a 4 Plex? Did you get a degree and now make six figures a year? Keep going backwards to get where you are now. Reverse engineer every step. Timer starts... Now.

Awesome! If you took this journaling exercise seriously, then you now have a game plan. This is your outline, your business plan, the start of your own personal playbook. With enough hard work and consistency, in ten years, you will be a completely different person, leaving the old you in the dust. Keep perfecting your playbook, no matter how crazy it sounds, because, as Steve Jobs puts it, "the people who are crazy enough to think they can change the world, are the ones who do."

"Here's to the crazy ones. The misfits. The rebels. The troublemakers. The round pegs in the square holes. The ones who see things differently. They're not fond of rules. And they have no respect for the status quo. You can quote them, disagree with them, glorify or vilify them. About the only thing you can't do is ignore them. Because they change things. They push the human race forward. And while some may see them as the crazy ones, we see genius. Because the people who are crazy enough to think they can change the world, are the ones who do."

—Steve Jobs

LETTING IT ALL OUT ON PAPER WILL **IMPROVE** ALL ASPECTS OF YOUR LIFE.

CHAPTER 3: MEDITATION

"In the stillness of meditation, you will find the power to manifest your true self."

—Deepak Chopra

Interstellar travelers, now that we've cleared some more space in your minds, let's clear even more space by diving into the transformative practice of meditation. Meditation traces its origins to ancient Earthling cultures like India and China, where it was initially practiced as part of religious traditions or to enhance well-being. Over time, meditation transcended geographical boundaries, and today, individuals from all corners of the world embrace it to attain inner calmness, heightened concentration, and a sense of contentment. This is especially true for accomplished Earthlings, who know that if you learn how to master your mind, you can master your life. The remarkable power of meditation—an ancient practice connecting beings across space and time, meditation is a practice that unlocks the boundless potential within you, allowing you to chart a course toward success on this extraordinary planet called Earth.

THE BENEFITS OF MEDITATION

Remember that a positive attitude is more than just a fleeting sentiment; it's a dynamic force that sets off a cascade of positive thoughts, leading to transformative events and outcomes. Like a spark igniting a fire, **a positive attitude becomes the catalyst for achieving extraordinary results.** As you integrate meditation into your daily life, you'll witness how this positivity radiates, touching every aspect of your being and those around you. Allow meditation to be your guiding light, illuminating the way forward and unveiling the brilliance that resides within.

SUCCESSFUL EARTHLINGS WHO MEDITATE

Meditation is a universal tool embraced by Earthlings from various walks of life who seek to unlock their potential.

Here are some notable examples:

David Lynch: The renowned filmmaker not only creates thought-provoking films but also encourages others to explore the depths of their consciousness through meditation.

Elon Musk: Amidst his busy schedule of spearheading groundbreaking technologies, he has publicly spoken about how meditation helps him maintain clarity and focus in his ambitious endeavors.

Bob Ross: The American painter and television host credited his daily meditation practice for helping him stay centered and focused in his creative process.

Russell Simmons: The co-founder of Def Jam Recordings, Simmons has credited his daily meditation practice for helping him to thrive in his business endeavors.

Jerry Seinfeld: The comedian and actor has talked about how his daily meditation practice helps him maintain a clear mind when performing.

LeBron James: The basketball star attributes part of his success on and off the court to his meditation routine. By cultivating a peaceful mind, he harnesses his mental strength and maintains a competitive edge.

These examples demonstrate how meditation is not confined to any specific sphere; it's a universal tool embraced by Earthlings from various walks of life who seek to unlock their potential.

Just as Earthlings have learned different ways to meditate from various cultures and traditions, you too can explore these methods. Some people meditate in silence, some listen to sounds, and others meditate while walking. There are many ways to meditate, but the goal is always the same: to clear the mind and feel calm, happy, and peaceful.

A positive attitude causes a chain reaction of positive thoughts, events, and outcomes. It is a catalyst that sparks extraordinary results. You must learn to trust that there is a future waiting for you that is beyond what you might be able to grasp at this present moment. Don't adapt to the energy in the room; influence the energy in the room. **Attitudes are contagious, so make yours worth catching.**

Remember that investing time in yourself is the greatest gift you can give yourself.

CHALLENGE #3: MEDITATION 101 – STEP OUT OF YOUR COMFORT ZONE

Meditation doesn't have to be intimidating or overly serious. It's simply about creating space to pause, breathe, and observe. But here's the twist: we're going to make it an adventure. This challenge will teach you the basics of meditation while pushing you to explore it in unexpected ways. Ready to step out of your comfort zone?

The Basics: How to Meditate

1. **Find Your Anchor:** Sit comfortably, close your eyes, and take a deep breath. Focus on your breath as it flows in and out. This is your anchor—a simple point of focus to return to whenever your mind wanders.

2. **Observe Without Judgment:** Let your thoughts drift like clouds across the sky. Notice them, but don't get caught up. Gently guide your attention back to your breath whenever you feel distracted.

3. **Start Small:** Begin with just 10 minutes. You don't need to empty your mind or achieve perfection. Meditation is a practice, not a performance.

Your Mission: Break the Mold

Now that you know the basics, it's time to shake things up. Meditation isn't just about sitting still—it's about exploring new ways to connect with yourself and the world around you.

1. **Meditate in Motion:** Take your meditation on the road. Walk slowly through your neighborhood, a park, or even a busy street. Focus on your breath and the rhythm of your steps. Notice how movement changes your awareness.

2. **Meditate Somewhere Unusual:** Step out of your comfort zone—literally. Meditate in a place you'd never normally go: a library, a coffee shop, a parking lot, or even a crowded subway. Sit quietly, close your eyes, and tune into the sounds and energy around you. How does it feel

to be still in the midst of chaos?

3. **Nature Immersion:** Find three different outdoor spots today—a park bench, a patch of grass, or under a tree. Spend 10 minutes in each place, focusing on your breath and listening deeply to the sounds around you. Write down how each spot feels different.

Push Yourself Further

- **Silent Observation:** Go to a public space—a mall, a train station, or a busy street. Sit quietly and observe the people around you without judgment. Notice their movements, expressions, and energy. How does it feel to witness life without participating?

- **Meditate with a Stranger:** If you're feeling bold, ask a friend, family member, or even a stranger to meditate with you for 10 minutes. Share the experience and discuss what you noticed afterward.

Reflect and Journal

After each meditation session, grab your journal and answer these questions:

- Where did you meditate, and how did it feel to step out of your comfort zone?
- What did you notice about your thoughts, emotions, or surroundings?
- Did anything surprise you or challenge your expectations?

Why This Matters

Meditation isn't just about finding peace—it's about breaking patterns, exploring new perspectives, and embracing the unexpected. By stepping out of your comfort zone, you'll discover that stillness can be found anywhere, even in the most unlikely places. This is your chance to shake up your routine, connect with the world around you, and see yourself in a new light.

CHAPTER 4: HABITS

"Every action you take is a vote for the type of person you wish to become."

—James Clear

L et's talk about something that's absolutely central to the lives of Earthlings—habits! You see, habits are like the threads that weave the story of their lives, holding together the intricate tapestry of their daily existence.

Now, imagine us, keen observers from the stars, gazing upon the Earthlings and their curious ways. What strikes us most is their deep reliance on these things called 'habits.' It's almost like a secret force, subtle yet as unyielding as gravity itself. **These habits are the foundations of their routines, the guiding lights for their actions, and, believe it or not, the very architects of their destinies.**

So, fellow explorers, as we embark on this voyage into the realm of habits, we're diving headfirst into the heart of human behavior. Get ready to unearth the incredible potential hidden within the tiniest tweaks—small changes that can lead to colossal transformations.

EARTHLING TERMS
MADE SIMPLE
HABITS

: Habits are things we do over and over without really thinking about them. They're like automatic actions. Imagine if you always tie your shoelaces the same way or eat your breakfast at the same time every day. Those are habits! Some habits are helpful, like brushing your teeth, and some might not be so good, like checking your phone too much or smoking.

Just like how you don't have to think hard about riding your bike once you've learned, your brain remembers how to do things because of habits. Some habits are like good friends that help you, like remembering to wash your hands before eating. But sometimes, there are habits that might not be very helpful, like turning to social media to numb a bad day.

Habits are like your brain's super-sneaky AI assistants. They help you per-form tasks automatically, without draining your mental energy, which frees up brainpower for new challenges. For example, if you have a habit of zoning out during small talk or reaching for that extra snack on tough days, these automatic behaviors kick in, guiding you to do what you've done before in similar situations. But here's the exciting part: you can re-program these habits! Just like teaching an AI a new task, you can train your brain to adopt healthier habits, which means you can break old pat-terns and create new ones that make you feel awesome.

Now, the trick to changing a bad habit is to make it a bit more of a hassle. Let's say you can't resist checking your phone and diving into the endless scroll of social media. Here's an idea: grab a cheap phone exclusively for social media, one that's not connected to any service. Now, you'll need to physically connect to Wi-Fi on a separate device just to indulge in some doom scrolling. That extra step makes the habit less enticing because it's more work.

When you make habits less accessible, you'll find yourself doing them less often.

And guess what? The same principle applies when you're building new good habits. You want to make them so easy that you'll stick with them, even on days when you're not feeling it. The key is to integrate these habits seamlessly into your daily routine. Habits thrive when they flow with your life. For instance, if you want to read and journal more, keep them in your bag so you can do them whenever you have a spare moment. Need to floss your teeth regularly? Keep disposable floss in your car for those quick flossing sessions when you're stuck in traffic. Make the good habits easy to accomplish and the not-so-good ones a bit of a hassle, and you'll witness a dramatic change in your life. Design your world to make it easy to do what's best for you.

Okay, let's bring one of my favorite authors to the party! Ever heard of James Clear? He's a super-smart Earthling who wrote a book called Atomic Habits. Now, he's got a really cool take on habits. He calls them the 'compound interest of self-improvement.' Picture it like this: just as your savings grow over time thanks to interest, those small choices you make every day are like little investments that shape who you become. It's like creating a masterpiece of yourself one tiny brushstroke at a time. (Alternately, if you make poor choices and adopt inferior habits, you could wind up with a self-portrait that looks like a bad Jackson Pollock.)

Now, let's dive into something else James Clear talks about—habit stacking. Imagine pairing a new habit with something you're already doing. For instance, if you're on a mission to become an early riser, here's a trick: put your phone across the room with a book you're eager to read. When your alarm goes off, you're forced to get up to turn it off, and while you're at it, grab the book and head outside to start reading. You've just stacked a new habit onto your early rising routine. This makes learning new habits much easier as it also helps you get up and start moving.

Here's some more good advice from Clear. Vague habits like "eat healthier" or "go to the gym more often" don't stick. Why? Because they lack specifics. To make them stick, you've got to be crystal clear about how you'll make them happen. Instead of saying, "I'll eat healthier" try "I will cut out sugars and replace all sweets with fruit." Or instead of "I'll go to the gym more" say "After I finish work, I'll head straight to the gym for a 30-minute workout." Being specific about when and where your new habit kicks in is the secret sauce for building lasting habits.

Now, here's a pro tip to get better at this: grab the book *Atomic Habits*, a highlighter, and a journal. Trust me, this book can transform your life just like it did mine.

And here's something cool to remember: Habits can either be your secret weapons for success or ticking time bombs holding you back. If you've struggled with habits on other planets, you're in luck because a new environment is like a fresh canvas for building new, positive habits. Embrace it and remember humans are also given this chance, though they might not realize it.

CHALLENGE #4: TRANSFORM YOUR HABITS

Now that you've learned about the power of habits, it's time to put that knowledge into action. This challenge will help you build one new positive habit and break one unhelpful habit using the principles we've discussed.

Step 1: Build a New Habit

1. **Choose a Habit:** Pick one small, positive habit you'd like to build. For example:

   - Drink a glass of water first thing in the morning.
   - Read for 10 minutes before bed.
   - Take a 5-minute walk after lunch.

2. **Make It Easy:** Use habit stacking to tie your new habit to something you already do. For example:

   - *"After I brush my teeth in the morning, I'll drink a glass of water."*
   - *"After I turn off the TV at night, I'll read for 10 minutes."*

3. **Track Your Progress:** Use a journal, app, or calendar to mark each day you successfully complete your new habit. Celebrate small wins to stay motivated.

Step 2: Break an Unhelpful Habit

1. **Identify the Habit:** Choose one habit you'd like to break. For example:

   - Scrolling social media before bed.
   - Snacking on junk food while watching TV.
   - Procrastinating on important tasks.

2. **Make It Harder:** Add friction to the habit to make it less appealing. For example:

   - Move your phone charger to another room so you can't scroll in bed.
   - Keep unhealthy snacks out of the house or in a hard-to-reach place.
   - Set a timer for 5 minutes and commit to starting

your task, even if you don't feel like it.

3. **Replace It:** Swap the unhelpful habit with a healthier alternative. For example:

- Instead of scrolling before bed, read a book or listen to calming music.
- Instead of snacking on junk food, keep cut-up veggies or fruit within reach.
- Instead of procrastinating, break your task into smaller, manageable steps.

Step 3: Reflect and Adjust

At the end of the week, take 10 minutes to journal on your progress. Ask yourself:

- How did it feel to build a new habit? What worked, and what didn't?
- What challenges did you face in breaking the unhelpful habit? How can you make it easier next week?
- What's one small adjustment you can make to improve your results?

Why This Matters

Habits are the building blocks of your life. By intentionally designing your habits, you can create a life that aligns with your goals and values. Remember, small changes compound over time, leading to massive transformations.

.

CAN YOU
BELIEVE SOME
EARTHLINGS
SPEND
8-12 HOURS
A DAY
LOOKING INTO
THIS THING?

CHAPTER 5: ENVIRONMENT

"The environment is in us, not outside of us. The trees are our lungs, the rivers our bloodstream. We are all interconnected, and what you do to the environment, ultimately you do to yourself."
—Native American Proverb

By now, you've navigated through the bustling streets, serene parks, and diverse dwellings of Earth, observing the countless ways Earthlings interact with their surroundings. As an interstellar visitor, the concept of 'environment' might strike you as a mere background to daily activities. Yet, on Earth, the spaces we inhabit profoundly shape our lives, subtly steering our behaviors and moods without our conscious awareness. Just as a gardener tends their garden, ensuring that each plant has the right conditions to thrive, we too must tend to our living spaces to cultivate a life of fulfillment and achievement.

Imagine this: On your planet, environments might be uniformly optimized for efficiency—every tool and setting engineered for function. Here, however, Earthlings often find themselves in spaces cluttered not just with objects but with hidden influences, each tugging at their emotions, draining their energy, or uplifting their spirits.

Your living space, for instance, might double as a relaxation zone and a work hub, mingling rest with productivity. This overlap blurs the boundaries that keep life's rhythms harmonious. Understanding and reshaping these spaces transforms mere existence into thriving—a crucial lesson for any being seeking success on this vibrant but complex planet.

Consider how Earthlings construct their surroundings to foster habits of health and focus. For example, picture your bedroom. If it also serves as your TV room and the place where you isolate yourself during moments of a breakdown, it's unlikely that you'll find peace and rest there. In fact, you may even start to dread spending time in that room. Or perhaps your dining room table doubles as your workspace. This arrangement hinders productivity and creates an imbalance of work and home life where you can find it difficult to start (or stop) working. The key to optimizing your living space is to assign a specific purpose to each area. As James Clear puts it, "One space, one use."

Efficient Earthlings structure their lives in a way that minimizes the need for extraordinary willpower or self-control. For instance, those who struggle with unhealthy eating habits might remove tempting junk food from their homes, replacing it with healthier options like fresh fruits or vegetables readily at hand.

Creating an optimal environment goes beyond mere physical space—it encompasses the people around you, the sensory experiences you allow, and the routines you establish. If social distractions impede your ability to focus on personal priorities, it may be necessary to reevaluate and adjust your social interactions. This concept mirrors the careful selection of your crew members on a space mission, where each individual's role and behavior are aligned with the mission's success. A truly disciplined Earthling, or in your case, a savvy extraterrestrial, creates a habitat that not only avoids unnecessary distractions but also actively propels them towards personal growth and accomplishment.

Let's explore more deeply how you can actively design your environment to support your Earthly endeavors:

- **Visual Harmony:** Consider the visual elements of your surroundings. Earthlings often underestimate the psychological impact of visual clutter. Streamline your living and working areas to reduce clutter, which can help reduce stress and improve focus. A minimalist approach encourages a calmer, more focused state of mind.

- **Sensory Details:** Pay attention to the sensory details of your environment. The right amount of lighting, comfortable temperatures, and minimal noise can significantly enhance your ability to concentrate and enjoy your daily activities. For instance, if you find natural light uplifting, position your workspace to maximize exposure to daylight.

- **Technology Zones:** Designate specific zones for technology use. Many Earthlings struggle with digital devices being everywhere, which can disrupt sleep and personal interactions. By creating tech-free zones, especially in bedrooms and dining areas, you will cultivate healthier habits around device usage.

CHALLENGE #5: DESIGN YOUR IDEAL ENVIRONMENT

Your surroundings have a powerful impact on your mood, focus, and habits. This challenge will help you create a space that supports your goals and well-being.

Step 1: Conduct an Environmental Audit

Spend a day observing how you use each area of your home. Ask yourself:

1. Does this space have a clear purpose?
2. How do I feel when I'm in this space?
3. Are there distractions or clutter that drain my energy?

Step 2: Redesign for Purpose

Assign one specific purpose to each space. For example:

1. Turn a corner of your living room into a reading nook.
2. Designate your dining table as a tech-free zone for meals and conversations.
3. Create a dedicated workspace that's separate from relaxation areas.
4. Remove items that don't align with the purpose of the space (e.g., work materials from your bedroom or trinkets and distractions that clutter your desk).

Step 3: Optimize Sensory Details

Lighting: Maximize natural light where possible. Use warm, soft lighting in relaxation areas and bright, focused lighting in workspaces.

Sound: Reduce noise distractions with rugs, curtains, or white noise machines.

Comfort: Adjust the temperature and add cozy elements like cushions or blankets to make the space inviting.

Step 4: Set Technology Boundaries

Designate tech-free zones, such as your bedroom or dining area, and set up a charging station outside these spaces to limit device use. By creating these boundaries, you may notice improvements in your sleep, focus, and personal interactions.

Step 5: Reflect and Adjust

After a week, journal on the changes:
1. How do your redesigned spaces make you feel?
2. Have your habits or productivity improved?
3. What small tweaks can you make to further enhance your environment?

Why This Matters

Your environment is more than just a backdrop—it's a tool for shaping your habits, mood, and success. By intentionally designing your space, you create a foundation for a more focused, balanced, and fulfilling life. But this isn't a one-time task. Just like Earth itself, your environment will continue to evolve with you. Revisit this challenge periodically to ensure your surroundings align with your needs, goals, and values. Even subtle changes—like repositioning furniture for better light or adding a touch of greenery—can ripple out to create profound effects on your daily life.

CHAPTER 6: AFFIRMATIONS

"Be kind to those who effect your mind."
—Christian Bland

CHANGING HOW YOU SPEAK TO YOURSELF

E very day, Earthlings have countless thoughts running through their minds. These thoughts, or "self-talk," greatly influence how they feel and what they do. Now, imagine turning these thoughts into supportive messages, much like the encouraging words one might hear from a good friend. That's the power of affirmations.

Think of it like this: you have a tiny friend who lives in your head, and this friend listens to everything you think about yourself. If you say, "I'm not good at this," your tiny friend believes it. But if you say, "I can do this," your friend believes that too! Affirmations are like giving your tiny friend some really nice things to believe about you. When you say kind things about yourself, like "I am smart" or "I am kind," your tiny friend starts to believe these nice things, and, because this tiny friend is you, so do you!

When I refer to affirmations, I'm essentially talking about improving the way you speak to yourself. Your brain can't distinguish between external criticism and your internal dialogue. Consider your worst enemy—it's quite possible you've spoken to yourself even more harshly than they ever have to you. Using affirmations isn't about deceiving yourself; it's about being mindful of the ongoing narrative in your mind and recognizing the actual words you're using to address yourself.

It's astonishing how many Earthlings are oblivious to the severity of their negative self-talk. One effective method to counteract this is by practicing positive affirmations. (See the exercise at the end of this chapter). Each time you catch yourself making a negative remark about yourself, consciously counter it by affirming five positive things. This practice isn't just an exercise in self-praise; it's a crucial step in transforming your internal dialogue to foster a healthier, more supportive mindset.

In my early years, I attended a challenging public school surrounded by classmates who often carried heavy traumas from home. This environment was a breeding ground for negativity, and it wasn't long before I internalized it myself. One phrase that stuck with me during those times was, "I hate God." For me, it wasn't about venting anger toward religion itself—it was a raw reflection of my frustration and helplessness, stemming from the feeling of being forced into a belief system I didn't fully understand or embrace.

This harsh phrase became a relentless loop in my mind, resurfacing constantly and adding to my stress and unhappiness. One day, I decided I had enough. Determined to change this negative loop, I countered each occurrence of the phrase with a positive one. Whenever the old, harsh phrase came to mind, I would instead say "Love God" five times. This wasn't about religion or preaching—it was about changing a harmful narrative into a positive one. This practice, simple as it might sound, was transformative. It not only broke the cycle but also dramatically shifted my outlook. This experience taught me a powerful lesson: If you find yourself trapped in a cycle of negative self-talk, consciously replacing it with something positive and repeating it multiple times can truly make a significant difference.

Many young Earthlings don't realize how their upbringing shapes their self-perception and behavior well into adulthood. Traumas from unstable or unloving homes can manifest in behaviors that sometimes last a lifetime. Learning the art of positive self-talk early on is crucial. It equips you to handle life's challenges more effectively and fosters a resilient, supportive mindset.

Life often seems to teach us lessons through repetition. It's easy to feel victimized by recurring problems, but each challenge is an opportunity to grow. Using affirmations turns these challenges into stepping stones towards a stronger self. Affirmations are more than just feel-good statements; they're a practice of self-empowerment. By choosing to speak kindly to yourself, you influence your inner narrative, which in turn affects your reality.

Give affirmations a try for just one week, and I promise, you'll see a change in your life. They might seem simple, but as unlikely as it might seem, they work.

Remember, the little friend in your head, your inner voice, is always listening. You get to decide whether this voice is going to be a good friend or not. Every time you say something positive about yourself, you're helping build a friendship with yourself that will make you feel stronger and more confident.

As you keep using affirmations, be kind and patient with yourself. Changing how you think doesn't happen quickly. Every positive thing you say is like planting a seed in your mind. Over time, with care and regular positive thoughts, these seeds grow into a garden of good feelings.

Your words are very powerful—use them to build the life you want.

CHALLENGE #6: TRANSFORM YOUR SELF-TALK WITH AFFIRMATIONS

This challenge will help you replace negative self-talk with positive affirmations, creating a kinder, more supportive inner dialogue.

Step 1: Choose Your Affirmations

Write down 3–5 positive statements that reflect the qualities or goals you want to focus on. For example:

- "I am confident and capable."
- "I am kind to myself and others."
- "I am resilient and can handle any challenge."

Make sure your affirmations feel personal and meaningful to you.

Step 2: Make It a Daily Practice

- Set aside 5–10 minutes each morning to recite your affirmations. Say them out loud with conviction, as if you already believe them.
- Use a mirror to look into your own eyes while speaking your affirmations. This makes the practice more powerful and personal.

Step 3: Counter Negative Thoughts

- Throughout the day, pay attention to your self-talk. When you catch yourself thinking something negative, immediately replace it with one of your affirmations.
- For example, if you think, "I'm not good enough," counter it with, "I am worthy and capable."

Step 4: Integrate Affirmations into Your Routine

- Say your affirmations during everyday activities, like brushing your teeth, driving, or taking a walk. This helps make positive thinking a natural part of your day.
- Write your affirmations on sticky notes and place them where you'll see them often—on your mirror, computer, or fridge.

Step 5: Reflect and Adjust

At the end of the week, journal on how the practice has impacted your mood and mindset. Ask yourself:

- Do I feel more confident or optimistic?
- Which affirmations resonated most with me?
- Are there new affirmations I'd like to add or adjust?

Why This Matters

Your inner dialogue shapes how you see yourself and the world. By practicing affirmations, you're planting seeds of positivity that will grow into confidence, resilience, and self-love. Over time, these small shifts in your self-talk can lead to profound changes in your life.

CHAPTER 7: MOVEMENT

"Take care of your body. It's the only place you have to live."
—Jim Rohn

It didn't take me long to realize how absurd it is that Earthlings are given incredible bodies capable of amazing physical feats yet, for some reason, the majority of this planet chooses to sit all day, staring at screens, letting their physical potential go to waste. I don't think I'll ever understand why; Earthlings are some strange beings.

You have a full 24 hours each day on this planet, and dedicating at least one of those hours to movement should always be a priority. The reason is simple: it's all about maintaining your daily energy levels. It's no secret that Earthlings who engage in regular physical activity tend to have higher energy levels compared to those who spend their days sitting at desks or lounging on the couch.

Studies have revealed a concerning fact: a staggering 95% of Earthlings over the age of 30 will never experience the thrill of sprinting or jumping again in their lifetime. Isn't that a rather disheartening thought? If you take a look around, you'll notice that many Earthlings exhibit signs of weakness and fragility, often accompanied by low energy levels and a dependency on stimulants like caffeine or doctor-prescribed medications. However, with just a little extra effort, you can easily stand out and excel on this planet because the majority of its inhabitants are not as physically active as they could be. This is why prioritizing movement is essential to succeeding here on Earth, whether it involves running, biking, weightlifting, martial arts, hiking, or any other physical activity that suits your preferences.

But here's the key: set a goal to consistently push beyond your comfort zone during your movement sessions. I've encountered countless Earthlings who claim that their job involves physical activity, such as lifting objects or climbing stairs throughout the day. While this is a form of active movement, it's primarily part of your job routine. The real work begins during your free time when you make a deliberate effort to schedule a time and place to challenge yourself physically, enhancing your stamina for the future. Train your brain and make it a habit that when you are at your breaking point, just take one step farther than you did the day before. You can do anything for 15 more seconds—just push a little bit harder each day, and within a year, your body will be unrecognizable.

I was not gifted with a body that would break world records, but I was given an opportunity to start fresh on this planet. I knew that I didn't want to be the slowest, and I saw how much work needed to be put in to become the fastest. In my early years, I knew that if I worked harder than the average Earthling, I could keep up with most naturally gifted ones. I tried many different sports but never felt like I fit in with the average jock. It wasn't until I started training in the most dominant martial art on this planet, Jiu-Jitsu, that I saw dramatic improvement over time. The more I attended class, the better I got. The more I trained my body— running, lifting weights, stretching, doing yoga—the more training my body could handle. A stronger, healthier body means better performance in class. As Tim Notke says, "Hard work beats talent when talent doesn't work hard."

To achieve success on this planet, you must continually push your limits. Trust me, in the long run, regular physical activity will sharpen both your mind and body, instilling a sense of confidence that enables you to tackle any challenge that comes your way. This kind of self-assuredness is what you should aim for each morning, waking up strong and ready to face the day. There's nothing worse than beginning a challenging day unsure of your capabilities or relying on sugary, caffeine-laden energy drinks or coffee just to make it through. These beverages are nothing more than crutches that provide a temporary, false sense of confidence. When movement becomes a priority, boundless energy becomes inevitable.

Keep in mind that wealth and health go hand in hand. To enjoy a healthy life, you need the time and energy to pursue great endeavors, and wealth is far more enjoyable when you are in good health.

CHALLENGE #7: MOVE MORE, EVERY DAY

This challenge will help you incorporate movement into your daily routine while encouraging you to step outside and explore. The goal is to make physical activity a natural part of your day, so you can build energy, strength, and confidence.

Step 1: Start Small

- Take the Stairs: Whenever possible, choose stairs over elevators or escalators. It's a simple way to get your heart pumping and strengthen your legs.
- Park Further Away: When driving, park at the far end of the parking lot. Those extra steps add up over time!

Step 2: Sneak in Movement

- Walk and Talk: Turn phone calls or meetings into walking sessions. Stroll around your home, office, or a nearby park while you chat.
- Desk Exercises: Try chair squats, desk push-ups, or calf lifts while working. These small movements keep your body active even when you're stuck at your desk.

Step 3: Add Intensity

- 10 Bodyweight Squats: Every hour, stand up and do 10 squats. These "exercise snacks" are quick but powerful boosts for your energy and metabolism.
- Stretch Breaks: Set a timer to remind yourself to stretch every hour. Reach for the ceiling, touch your toes, or do side bends to keep your muscles loose and relaxed.

Step 4: Explore Active Transportation

- If possible, walk, bike, or skate to your destinations instead of driving. It's a great way to stay active while reducing your carbon footprint.

Step 5: The Outdoor Adventure Challenge

This is your chance to step outside your comfort zone and connect with nature:

- Choose Your Adventure: Pick one outdoor activity to try this week. It could be hiking a new trail, biking through your neighborhood, trying outdoor yoga in a park, or even just taking a long walk in an area you've never explored before.
- Set a Goal: Give yourself a small challenge to make it fun. For example:
- Hike to a scenic viewpoint and take a photo.
- Bike to a local landmark or café you've never visited.
- Do 10 minutes of stretching or yoga in a quiet outdoor spot.
- Reflect: After your adventure, jot down a few thoughts. How did it feel to move your body in a new environment? What did you notice about your surroundings?

Step 6: Reflect and Level Up

At the end of the week, journal on your progress:

- Which activities felt easiest to incorporate?
- How did adding movement impact your energy and mood?
- What's one new way you can challenge yourself next week?

Why This Matters

Movement isn't just about fitness—it's about vitality, confidence, and enjoying life to the fullest. By making small changes to your daily routine and stepping outside to explore, you'll build a stronger, healthier body and mind. Remember, every step counts!

CHAPTER 8: FOOD

"If you can control your stomach, you can control the world..." —John P. Rosales

Food products on this planet are often not made for nutritional value. They are designed to look and taste good to consumers. On Earth, especially in the United States, millions of dollars are spent testing food products to achieve the perfect crunch or the ideal color to appeal to Earthlings' senses. Processed food here is more about profit than nutrition. The main goal is, "What products can we create to ensure more people keep buying our products?"

Depending on which star system you come from, food might mean something completely different to you. Some aliens don't even need to eat because their planet supplies them with nutrients through the air as they sleep and breathe, while others must excavate their planet for sustenance. Food on this planet, as you're probably aware, plays a vital role in optimizing both the physical and mental well-being of Earthlings. So does the concept of intermittent fasting, which involves abstaining from eating for certain periods. The key here is finding balance between meeting the body's essential requirements for proper functioning and cultivating a healthy connection with the food you consume.

UNDERSTANDING EARTH'S FOOD SYSTEM

Earthlings have a diverse array of food available to them, ranging from fresh, whole foods to highly processed products. Fresh foods include fruits, vegetables, grains, proteins, and healthy fats—essentially, anything that was once alive or grew from the earth's soil. These foods provide crucial nutrients for the body, helping it thrive and maintain optimal health.

On the other hand, processed foods tell a different story. Packaged snacks, frozen meals, sugary breakfast cereals, and processed meats like bacon, sausage, jerky, and hot dogs are often filled with additives, preservatives, and artificial ingredients. Despite the flashy branding and marketing, these products offer little to no nutritional value. In fact, many processed foods can be harmful to your health, contributing to issues like obesity, heart disease, and diabetes. While they may be convenient and tempting, it's important to recognize that they are highly engineered and far removed from the natural, nourishing foods our bodies need.

Your daily intake should encompass a variety of nutrients. Aim to include a colorful assortment of fruits and vegetables, whole grains, lean proteins, and healthy fats—in other words, strive to 'eat the rainbow.' These components work in harmony to fuel your body and maintain its peak performance. (And just because it's good for you doesn't mean it can't also be delicious: see my recipes at the end of the chapter.)

A helpful guideline to remember is: if it wasn't once alive, try to avoid eating it. This means focusing on natural, whole foods that come from living sources. Fruits, vegetables, grains, nuts, seeds, and proteins like lean meat and fish are all examples of foods that were once alive. These nutrient-dense options provide the essential fuel your body needs to function at its best.

Simple Steps to Implement This:

1. **Choose Whole Foods:** When shopping, opt for foods in their natural state. This includes fresh produce, whole grains, and unprocessed proteins. If it comes in a package, it is most likely processed.

2. **Read Labels:** If you do buy packaged foods, read the ingredient list. Avoid products with long lists of unrecognizable ingredients, which are often chemicals and preservatives.

3. **Plan Balanced Meals:** Each meal should include a mix of colorful fruits and vegetables, whole grains like brown rice or quinoa, lean proteins such as chicken or beans, and healthy fats like avocados or nuts.

4. **Cook Simple Recipes:** Preparing meals at home allows you to control what goes into your food. Try simple recipes that use whole ingredients. For example, a stir-fry with a variety of vegetables, some chicken, and a side of rice makes a nutritious and delicious meal.

5. **Snack Smart:** Keep healthy snacks on hand, like fresh fruit and nuts. These will keep you satisfied between meals and provide a steady source of energy.

By following these simple steps, you can easily incorporate nutrient-rich, once-alive foods into your diet. Not only will this help you maintain high energy levels and overall health, but you'll also find that these foods can be both delicious and satisfying. Eating well doesn't have to be complicated—focus on natural, whole foods, and your body will thank you.

EXPLORING INTERMITTENT FASTING

Intermittent fasting is a healthy Earthling strategy worth considering. This approach involves alternating between periods of eating and fasting, giving your digestive system a break. By allowing your body to focus on repair and rejuvenation during fasting periods, you can promote longevity and overall well-being.

One of the simplest ways to implement intermittent fasting is to align your eating schedule with your circadian rhythm, which means eating only during daylight hours. By doing this, you give your body the nighttime hours to properly digest and rest. This practice not only aids in digestion but also improves the quality of your sleep. Eating a big meal before bed forces your body to work on digestion at a slower pace, disrupting your sleep and leaving you feeling groggy and less productive the next day. To avoid this, aim to finish large meals at least two hours before going to bed.

Timing your meals can significantly affect your energy levels. Eating a substantial meal before attending a social event can leave you feeling sluggish because your body needs to expend energy to digest it. Instead, consider consuming something light, such as fruit or nuts, to provide a bit of fuel without draining your energy. This way, you can stay alert and focused during activities that demand stamina and concentration.

If you align your dietary choices with your body's needs, fasting can enhance your mood, boost brain function, and leave you with a surplus of energy. While it may require some courage, especially before social events where quick energy boosts like alcohol and stimulants are prevalent, adopting these strategies will help you optimize your time on Earth by relying on your body's natural abilities rather than temporary fixes.

Balance is the key. Eat for nourishment, not solely for pleasure. Be mindful of portion sizes and ensure that your food choices align with your health goals. Food should empower you, providing you with the energy and vitality needed to accomplish great things on this planet.

Here are a few tips to help you implement intermittent fasting and make the most out of this practice:

1. **Start Gradually:** If you're new to intermittent fasting,

start with a shorter fasting period, such as 12 hours, and gradually increase it as your body adjusts.

2. **Stay Hydrated:** Drink plenty of water throughout the day to stay hydrated. Sometimes when you think you are hungry, it's actually your body craving more water. Herbal teas are also good options during fasting periods.

3. **Listen to Your Body:** Pay attention to how your body responds to fasting. If you feel overly hungry or fatigued, adjust your eating window. It's important to ensure that fasting fits your body's needs and doesn't cause undue stress.

4. **Focus on Nutrient-Dense Foods:** When you break your fast, choose nutrient-dense foods that provide a balance of carbohydrates, proteins, and fats to fuel your body effectively. Sometimes your body craves food because it didn't get the proper nutrients it needed, and that signal of hunger is its way of saying, "I need more nutrients."

5. **Be Consistent:** Try to maintain a consistent eating and fasting schedule to help your body adapt to the routine. Consistency helps regulate your body's internal clock and optimizes the benefits of intermittent fasting.

With intermittent fasting you can harness the natural rhythms of your body to enhance your health and well-being. Remember, the goal is to nourish your body and mind, enabling you to thrive on this planet.

MINDFUL EATING PRACTICES

Here's another essential principle that healthy Earthlings practice: It's not just about what you eat, but also how you eat. The way you approach mealtime can have a significant impact on your overall health and well-being. Eating slowly allows you to truly enjoy the flavors, textures, and aromas of your food. When you take the time to savor each bite, you become more aware of what you're eating and how it makes you feel. This mindful approach can lead to greater satisfaction and prevent overeating. By slowing down, you give your body the time it needs to recognize feelings of fullness, helping you avoid consuming more than necessary.

Transforming your meals into a mindful experience involves being fully present while you eat. This means eliminating distractions such as TV, smartphones, or computers. Focus on the food in front of you, paying attention to its colors, smells, and flavors. Notice the different textures and chew your food thoroughly. This not only aids digestion but also allows you to appreciate the effort that went into preparing your meal.

Eating mindfully can enhance your physical digestion by breaking down food into smaller pieces, making it easier for your digestive system to process. This leads to better nutrient absorption and fewer digestive issues. Mindful eating also fosters a deeper appreciation of the nourishment you're providing your body, encouraging you to think about where your food comes from and the journey it took to reach your plate.

Creating a calm and pleasant atmosphere for your meals can further enhance your eating experience. Take a moment before you start eating to breathe deeply and express gratitude for your meal. Being mindful helps you tune into your body's hunger and fullness signals, allowing you to eat when you're hungry and stop when you're satisfied. This practice can prevent overeating and help you maintain a healthy relationship with food.

Remember, it's not just about the food you eat, but how you eat it that can make a significant difference in your health and well-being.

When I first arrived on Earth, the family that raised me and the education systems I attended were misled by inaccurate health information, notably the highly criticized and impractical "food pyramid." This misguided guidance led to poor nutrition, and as a result, I experienced malnutrition for the first 21 years of my life on this planet.

I vividly remember my school days, drinking soda and chocolate milk, and eating sugary breakfasts and fried foods daily. After graduating high school, my diet didn't improve—in fact, it got worse. Dollar burgers, fried potatoes, and often rice and beans with tortillas became my staple meals. Things took a further downturn when I reached the legal drinking age. Late-night meals after nights out drinking continued for another decade.

Eventually, I started developing stomach problems. I thought it was just something natural that happens as you age on this planet. Feeling increasingly unwell, I realized I had to make a change. My first drastic step was to stop eating and drink only water for a few days, then reintroduce foods to see how my body would react. I began with simple foods like carrots and apples, and when I had a decently cooked meal at a restaurant, I had a reaction. This cycle repeated until I could identify what foods I could tolerate and what I needed to avoid.

The simplest solution seemed to be seeking out healthier food options and cooking at home, but I was overwhelmed by the variety of food available. It quickly became apparent that much of what was marketed as "food" was actually a mix of chemicals designed for taste and appearance rather than health. Growing up in a generally poor environment, the easily accessible food products were just cheap, processed imitations.

Determined to improve my health, I started learning to cook simple, healthy meals that would fuel my body. One of my favorite discoveries was overnight oats, a quick and nutritious breakfast option that I could prepare the night before. Another go-to meal became rice and veggies cooked in a rice cooker—simple, satisfying, and packed with nutrients.

By prioritizing nutritious, whole foods, I was able to maintain high energy levels, improve my mood, get rid of the stomach problems, and enhance my overall well-being. I began to feel like a real athlete with a strong, resilient body. This balance allowed me to focus and engage more in the activities I enjoyed.

Understanding and optimizing your relationship with food is crucial for thriving on Earth. The food you choose to consume has a direct impact on your physical and mental well-being. By focusing on natural, whole foods and incorporating mindful eating practices, you can significantly improve your health and energy levels.

Remember that the food industry often prioritizes profit over nutrition, so it's essential to be mindful of your food choices. Opt for foods that were once alive, and strive to eat a colorful assortment of fruits, vegetables, whole grains, lean proteins, and healthy fats. Implementing simple strategies like intermittent fasting and mindful eating can further enhance your well-being.

Eating well doesn't have to be complicated. By making informed choices and taking control of your diet, you can nourish your body and mind, enabling you to reach your full potential on this planet. Let your journey with food be one of discovery and empowerment as you learn to fuel your body with the nutrients it needs to thrive.

CHALLENGE #8: NOURISH YOUR BODY WITH INTENTION

This challenge will help you take control of your diet by preparing simple, nutritious meals and exploring mindful eating practices. The goal is to fuel your body with whole, nourishing foods while developing a deeper connection to what you eat.

Step 1: Cook a New Meal from Scratch

- **Choose a Recipe:** Pick one new recipe to try this week. It could be one of the quick meals listed below or something entirely new. The key is to use whole, unprocessed ingredients.

- **Gather Your Ingredients:** Make a shopping list and visit your local market or grocery store to find fresh, colorful ingredients.

- **Cook with Intention:** As you prepare your meal, focus on the process. Notice the textures, smells, and colors of the ingredients. Enjoy the act of creating something nourishing for yourself.

- **Share or Reflect:** If possible, share your meal with someone else. If not, take a moment to reflect on the experience. How did it feel to cook something new? How did the meal taste compared to processed or premade foods?

Quick Meal Ideas:

1. **Overnight Oats:** Combine rolled oats with your choice of milk, a spoonful of yogurt, and toppings like fresh fruit, nuts, or seeds. Let it sit in the fridge overnight for a ready-to-eat breakfast.

2. **Rice and Veggies in a Rice Cooker:** Toss rice and chopped vegetables (carrots, broccoli, mushrooms, etc.) into a rice cooker and steam tray with water and a pinch of salt. Cook until tender for a simple, hands-off meal.

3. **Simple Smoothies:** Blend spinach, a banana, frozen

berries, and a splash of water or milk for a quick, nutrient-packed drink.

4. **Baked Sweet Potatoes:** Bake a sweet potato and top it with your choice of filling for a fiber-rich meal.

5. **Quinoa Salad:** Cook quinoa, let it cool, and mix it with chopped veggies, beans, and a extra virgin olive oil and lemon juice dressing.

Step 2: Practice Mindful Eating

- **Eliminate Distractions:** Turn off the TV, put away your phone, and focus solely on your meal.
- **Savor Each Bite:** Pay attention to the flavors, textures, and aromas of your food. Chew slowly and notice how your body responds.
- **Express Gratitude:** Before eating, take a moment to express gratitude for the nourishment in front of you.

Step 3: Reflect and Adjust

At the end of the week, journal on your experience:

- How did cooking a new meal from scratch feel? Did it change your relationship with food?
- What did you notice about your energy levels and mood when eating whole, unprocessed foods?
- What's one small change you can make to continue improving your diet?

Why This Matters

Food is more than fuel—it's a way to connect with your body, your environment, and the people around you. By cooking your own meals and eating mindfully, you take control of your health and well-being. This challenge is your first step toward building a healthier, more intentional relationship with food.

CHAPTER 9: READERS ARE LEADERS

"The man who does not read good books has no advantage over the man who cannot read them."

—Mark Twain

For some odd reason, here on Earth, the vast majority of wisdom and knowledge is contained in these things called books. These books are essentially a collection of thin pieces of wood pulp bound together and stamped with ink. Before the invention of the internet, books were the primary method for passing down knowledge from generation to generation. Even now, with all the digital advancements, there is substantial research indicating that reading from physical books tends to enhance comprehension and retention more effectively than reading from digital screens.

Think of reading not as a mundane task but as lifting weights for your brain. Your bookshelf? It's essentially a brain gym. This chapter might just be the most crucial in our exploration because, let's face it, we all need a bit of help now and then. The ability to read and research is key to navigating questions and challenges on this planet.

Feeling a bit lost or uninformed? Reading is a brilliant antidote. It's not just about processing words; it's about expanding your vocabulary, enhancing your spelling, and enriching your conversational skills. Worried about sounding mundane or repetitive? Reading infuses your dialogue with fresh, authentic perspectives, steering clear of the banal and the cliché.

Books are portals to new worlds, diverse cultures, and profound ideas. They offer you the chance to walk in someone else's shoes, understand different viewpoints, and develop empathy. Whether you're delving into fiction or non-fiction, each page turned is a step towards a more knowledgeable and well-rounded version of yourself. So, gear up for a journey through the limitless realms of human thought and creativity. Let's explore the immense power of reading and how to get better at it so you can transform your experience on this planet.

Now, let's talk about how to excel at reading. First, create the right environment. This could be anywhere—a cozy coffee shop, a peaceful park, or the comfort of your own home. Pop in some headphones and listen to instrumental music, like classical or lo-fi hip-hop—music that sounds smart to you. This simple cue helps signal your brain that it's time to focus and get into the reading zone.

Remember, marathon reading sessions aren't necessary. Just 15 minutes of focused reading can do wonders. Arm yourself with a highlighter to mark phrases that strike a chord. These highlights are not just reminders of where you left off; they're beacons guiding you back into the mindset you'd discovered during your last session.

Don't overwhelm yourself. Set aside specific times to read in your chosen environment, or "habit stack" your reading during everyday moments— like while waiting for food at a restaurant or on a lunch break. It's also important to have a well-balanced reading diet. Fiction offers an enjoyable escape, but books that focus on skills you want to improve will have a lasting impact. Unsure where to begin? Bestseller lists and the self-help section are great places to start (and don't forget the recommended reading list at the end of this book).

My own journey into reading began with Real Artists Don't Starve, a book that completely transformed my view on art with its engaging real-world stories. As an artist, I've always loved rags-to-riches stories and the underdog destined for failure, or the failure after failure that eventually led to enormous success. This was exactly the kind of story I needed to read to understand that all artists go through the same struggles, and the ones who come out on top are the ones who are resilient and push forward no matter what. I really think that the key to loving to read is to read books that you love. Follow your curiosity; it will lead you to all kinds of interesting places.

The fact that you're reading this now is a victory in itself. It shows you care. And remember, there's no rush. Sometimes a book might sit on my shelf for months before I pick it up again—life happens. But just like staying fit, consistency is what matters. For me, that means getting up before dawn to carve out precious reading time, or it simply won't happen.

Reading is one of the most powerful tools you have at your disposal. It opens doors to new ideas, helps you grow intellectually, and enhances your ability to communicate effectively. By adding regular reading into your routine, you can transform not only your knowledge base but also your overall perspective on life.

Remember, the goal is to read regularly and enjoy the process. Don't stress about the quantity; focus on the quality and the experience of immersing yourself in a good book. As you continue to read, you'll find your brain becoming more adept at processing information, enhancing your cognitive abilities and making you smarter. Think of reading as a workout for your brain, helping you to thrive on this planet by continually learning and expanding your mind.

READING IS ONE OF THE MOST POWERFUL TOOLS YOU HAVE AT YOUR DISPOSAL.

IT OPENS DOORS TO NEW IDEAS, HELPS YOU GROW INTELLECTUALLY AND ENHANCES YOUR ABILITY TO COMMUNICATE EFFECTIVELY.

CHALLENGE #9: EMBARK ON A READING ADVENTURE

This challenge will help you reignite your love for reading by exploring new genres and discovering books that inspire growth, curiosity, and imagination. The goal is to make reading an exciting and enriching part of your daily life.

Step 1: Visit Your Local Library

1. Walk or Bike There: Make the journey part of the adventure. Walk or ride your bike to your nearest public library.

2. Pick a "Choose Your Own Adventure" Book: Explore the fiction section and find a "Choose Your Own Adventure" book. These interactive stories are fun, engaging, and a great way to reconnect with the joy of reading.

3. Bonus: While you're there, sign up for a library card if you don't already have one. It's your passport to endless knowledge and stories.

Step 2: Explore a Bookstore

1. Find a Non-Fiction Book: Head to a local bookstore and browse the non-fiction section. Choose a book in a category that will help you learn a new skill or improve an area of your life—business, self-help, cooking, gardening, or anything that sparks your curiosity.

2. Ask for Recommendations: If you're unsure what to pick, ask a bookstore employee or fellow reader for suggestions. Sometimes the best books come from unexpected recommendations.

Step 3: Create a Reading Ritual

1. Set a Daily Reading Goal: Start with 10–15 minutes a day. Use this time to dive into your new books.

2. Create a Cozy Reading Nook: Find a comfortable

spot in your home where you can read without distractions. Add a cozy chair, good lighting, and maybe a blanket to make it inviting.

3. Pair Reading with Daily Activities: Read during your morning coffee, on your lunch break, or before bed. Make it a natural part of your routine.

Step 4: Reflect and Journal

At the end of the week, journal on your experience:

1. How did it feel to visit the library and bookstore? Did you discover anything surprising or exciting?

2. What did you enjoy about the "Choose Your Own Adventure" book? Did it bring back a sense of playfulness or curiosity?

3. What new skill or insight are you hoping to gain from your non-fiction book?

4. How can you make reading a regular part of your life moving forward?

Why This Matters

Reading is more than just a pastime—it's a way to expand your mind, explore new worlds, and grow as a person. By stepping out of your comfort zone and exploring different types of books, you'll rediscover the joy of reading and unlock new possibilities for learning and growth.

CHAPTER 10: SLEEP

"Sleep: where the mind heals and the spirit rejuvenates."
—Matthew Walker

As interstellar travelers navigating the complexities of life on this vibrant planet, you, my fellow beings, are about to learn one of Earth's most vital secrets: the science of sleep. Sleep impacts every aspect of well-being and is essential for success. It also affects your biology in surprising ways. For example, studies have shown that men who consistently get only five hours of sleep a night tend to have smaller testicles than those who enjoy seven hours or more. This lack of sleep can prematurely age a man by up to a decade in terms of his reproductive health. Similarly, insufficient sleep also impacts women's reproductive health, making this an essential issue for both genders.

On this remarkable planet, sleep is not merely a luxury but a biological necessity. Just as you harness energy from the stars, sleep is the cosmic energy source that fuels an Earthling's journey. During sleep, your mind process-es memories and harmonizes thoughts. An intricate dance of sleep cycles unfolds—a nightly choreography within the realm of dreams. REM (Rap-id Eye Movement) sleep, the stage of dreams, nurtures creativity and helps crystallize solutions to terrestrial challenges. Meanwhile, deep sleep re-pairs your body, bolstering your physical resilience for the forthcoming day.

But here's the twist: Poor sleep isn't just a footnote in the story of your life; it's the unexpected plot twist that can disrupt your narrative of success. Just as a bad meal before a social event can drain your energy, insufficient sleep distorts your day, hindering cognition, creativity, and even emotion-al stability. The mind that seeks to conquer Earth's feats must first surren-der to sleep's embrace, acknowledging its role as the catalyst of triumph.

THE BRAIN'S LEARNING AND MEMORY MECH-ANISM

It's not just about recuperation after learning; you also need sleep before acquiring new knowledge. Without it, your brain's memory circuits re-semble a soggy sponge, unable to soak up fresh information. In a study comparing individuals who enjoyed a full eight hours of sleep to those subjected to sleep deprivation, the sleep-deprived group exhibited a star-tling 40% reduction in their ability to create new memories.

The hippocampus, an informational gateway in your brain, is responsible for receiving and retaining new memories. In individuals who enjoy a full night's sleep, researchers have observed vibrant, learning-related activity within this region. In contrast, those deprived of sleep exhibit a stark ab-sence of significant brain activity, rendering their memory gateways inef-fective.

The quality of sleep you receive holds the key to enhancing memory and learning. Deep sleep stages feature powerful brainwaves accompanied by bursts of electrical activity called sleep spindles. These elements work in unison, shifting memories from a short-term, vulnerable state to a more secure, long-term storage site in the brain.

SLEEP'S IMPACT ON THE BODY

Insufficient sleep disrupts reproductive systems, cardiovascular health, and even immune function. Studies have revealed that losing just one hour of sleep can lead to a 24% increase in heart attacks, while gaining an extra hour results in a 21% reduction in heart attack rates. This pattern extends to car accidents, road traffic incidents, and even suicide rates.

Moreover, sleep deprivation profoundly affects the immune system. Natural killer cells, the body's immune agents, experience a 70% reduction in activity after a single night of sleep restricted to four hours. Short sleep duration is now strongly linked to various forms of cancer, including colorectal, prostate, and breast cancer. Nighttime shift work has even been classified as a probable carcinogen by the World Health Organization due to its disruptive effects on sleep-wake rhythms.

Sleep deprivation can alter the activity of hundreds of genes, impairing the immune system and increasing the promotion of tumors, chronic inflammation, and stress-related genes, ultimately contributing to cardiovascular disease.

REMEMBER THESE FACTS

Hitting the snooze button stresses out your cardiovascular system. Each time you snooze, your body enters multiple disrupted wake-sleep cycles, releasing stress hormones like cortisol and adrenaline. These hormones raise your heart rate and blood pressure, putting unnecessary strain on your heart. Over time, this interrupted sleep and constant stress response can lead to serious health issues, such as high blood pressure, heart disease, and even stroke.

Many people also turn to alcohol or marijuana, mistakenly believing they aid sleep. Alcohol is a sedative that induces drowsiness, not natural sleep, and disrupts your rest with frequent awakenings. It also suppresses REM sleep, which is crucial for emotional and mental well-being. Similarly, while marijuana might help you fall asleep, it blocks REM sleep, potentially increasing anxiety and depression over time.

Instead of relying on crutches like these, focus on managing your energy throughout the day. This allows your body to naturally recognize when it's time to sleep. After all, sleep is the most important tool in this playbook—mastering it should never depend on external aids.

THE CHALLENGE OF SLEEP

Sleep issues manifest in various forms, encompassing excessive, inadequate, or poor-quality sleep, and any of these can adversely affect your metabolism. Sleep problems intensify both mental and metabolic conditions. Insufficient sleep amplifies the challenges linked to depression, mania, anxiety, dementia, ADHD, and substance abuse disorders.

To thrive on this planet, sleep must be your number one priority. Sleep must be treated as a sport. When we don't get enough sleep, the following is likely to happen:

- Cognitive Impairment: Memory lapses, reduced creativity, and difficulty learning and problem-solving.
- Emotional Disturbances: Heightened irritability, mood swings, emotional reactivity, and a heightened susceptibility to stress and anxiety.
- Physical Health Issues: Elevated risk of various health problems, such as obesity, diabetes, heart disease, and weakened immune function.
- Mental Health Challenges: An increased likelihood of experiencing mood disorders like depression and anxiety.
- Decreased Productivity: Reduced work performance, productivity, and an increased risk of accidents, espe-

cially in tasks requiring focus and alertness.

- Memory Problems: Impaired memory consolidation, affecting your ability to retain and recall information.
- Impaired Motor Skills: Reduced coordination and slower reaction times, increasing the risk of accidents, particularly when driving.
- Hormonal Imbalances: Disruption of hormone regulation, leading to imbalances affecting appetite, metabolism, and overall health.
- Increased Pain Sensitivity: Greater sensitivity to pain and a reduced pain tolerance.
- Hallucinations and Psychosis: In severe cases of sleep deprivation, individuals may experience hallucinations and symptoms resembling psychosis.
- Impaired Immune Function: A weakened immune system response, making the body more vulnerable to infections.
- Altered Hormones and Appetite: Hormonal shifts can lead to increased appetite and cravings for unhealthy foods, contributing to weight gain.

I understand this might sound like a pharmaceutical ad at this point, but it's crucial to emphasize the immense impact of sleep on your well-being.

PRIORITIZING BETTER SLEEP

Let's shift away from the doom & gloom and focus on solutions. Prioritizing quality sleep becomes your primary mission. Consistency is key, with recommended sleep patterns of 7 to 9 hours each night for optimal health. Irregular sleep patterns, such as weekday sleep deprivation followed by weekend oversleeping, are linked to health risks like diabetes and obesity. Remember, you can't make up for lost sleep on subsequent nights; you must be consistently sleeping.

To enhance both the quantity and quality of your sleep, consider two fundamental principles: regularity and temperature. Establishing a consistent sleep schedule, with the same bedtime and wake-up time every day, serves as your anchor to solid sleep patterns. Additionally, maintaining a cooler bedroom environment, around 65 degrees Fahrenheit or 18 degrees Celsius, facilitates both falling asleep and staying asleep.

In closing, sleep isn't just a luxury; it's a biological necessity. It influences every facet of our well-being, from reproductive health to cognitive function and immune resilience. The erosion of sleep in modern society carries severe consequences for our health, safety, well-being, and education. It's high time to reclaim your right to a full night of rest, recognizing it as a potent elixir of life. In doing so, you'll regain your physical and mental vitality. Sleep is a partnership between you and the universe. As you prepare to venture into the chapters that unfold, remember that understanding and embracing the rhythm of sleep is your compass, guiding you toward the pinnacle of achievement.

CHALLENGE #10: MASTER YOUR SLEEP

This challenge will help you prioritize sleep and understand its profound impact on your energy, mood, and overall well-being. The goal is to establish a consistent sleep routine and track how it transforms your daily life.

Step 1: Set a Consistent Sleep Schedule

- Choose Your Bedtime and Wake-Up Time: Pick a bedtime and wake-up time that allows for 7–9 hours of sleep. Stick to this schedule every day, even on weekends.

- Create a Bedtime Ritual: Develop a relaxing routine to signal to your body that it's time to wind down. This could include reading, meditating, or taking a warm bath.

Step 2: Track Your Sleep

Keep a Sleep Journal. Each morning, write down:

- What time you went to bed and woke up.
- How many hours of sleep you got.
- How rested you feel on a scale of 1 to 10.
- Monitor Your Energy Levels: Throughout the day, note your energy levels, mood, and productivity. Are there patterns or changes as you stick to your sleep schedule?

Step 3: Optimize Your Sleep Environment

- Cool and Dark: Keep your bedroom around 65°F (18°C) and make it as dark as possible. Use blackout curtains or an eye mask if needed.

- Quiet and Calm: Reduce noise with earplugs or a white noise machine. Remove distractions like TVs or work-related items from your bedroom.

Step 4: Reflect and Adjust

At the end of the week, journal on your experience:

- How did sticking to a consistent sleep schedule feel? Did you notice changes in your energy or mood?

- What challenges did you face, and how can you overcome them?
- What's one small change you can make to improve your sleep even further?

Why This Matters

Sleep is the foundation of your physical, mental, and emotional well-being. By prioritizing consistent, high-quality sleep, you'll unlock higher energy levels, better focus, and a greater sense of balance in your life. This challenge is your first step toward mastering the art of sleep and reaping its countless benefits.

CHAPTER 11: SUNRISE RITUALS

"Every morning we are born again. What we do today is what matters most."

—Buddha

The rising sun on Earth signals more than just the start of a new day—it symbolizes the opportunity for a fresh beginning. As newcomers to this planet, you have the unique chance to embrace each sunrise as a reset button, just as wise Earthlings do. They recognize the power of the morning to set the tone for the rest of the day, using these early hours to prepare themselves mentally and physically for the challenges ahead. For high achievers on this planet, the early morning is a time to get ahead, work on personal projects, and enjoy a moment of peace before the world wakes up. Yet these early risers are not just out to gain a competitive edge; they seek a personal sanctuary where they can reflect, plan, and grow. This sacred time, free from the usual distractions, allows them to focus on what truly matters.

Imagine the world still asleep, and you're up, greeting the day with intention. These early hours offer a unique stillness, a break from the constant buzz of life. It's a moment to breathe, think clearly, and let your creativity flow without interruption. Whether you're reading a book, planning a new venture, or simply sitting with your thoughts, the early morning provides a rare opportunity for uninterrupted focus.

Embracing these early hours can feel almost rebellious. It's not about joining the hustle culture but about carving out time for yourself. In the quiet of dawn, you find a space where your thoughts can breathe, allowing for deeper reflection and creativity.

I have always struggled with the concept of a morning routine. The idea of waking up early and doing the same thing every day seemed daunting. However, I quickly realized the benefits of greeting the day before everyone else by observing the most successful people I worked for; as they all had a similar morning routine. One of them would have his entire family wear red glasses around sunset to block out any blue light to help prepare them for sleep once the sun fully set so they could be up at 5 am the next morning. While that might seem a bit extreme, another client of mine would go to sleep before midnight and be up around 7 am. Journaling and meditation were the first things they would do, followed by a workout. Then they would start work and get so much done that it all made sense why both these people were worth millions and in the best shape of their lives.

Once I decided to take on a similar routine, things really started to take shape in my life, including this book. I would think about my future self in these morning hours and how I could become that successful artist who escaped the rat race of life here on the planet. All I really wanted was to be able to afford quality nutrients and be able to invest in my dream projects. The only way to do this was to figure out a way to create more time in my life to create, and the morning routine was the key to unlocking the door to the future I wanted to live in. Now, I'm nowhere close to perfect; this did not happen overnight. Like any routine, if you fall off, it's hard to get back to it. Remember to be kind to yourself and give yourself the rest your body needs. But remember, you will only be in the exact same place with your goals if you keep sleeping in. Waking up early is a win that you should feel proud of accomplishing, just like finishing a tough workout. The future you deserve is in your hands. While the rest of the world is tucked away in their beds and snoozing their alarms, you can be up and at it, setting the stage for the day, and every task that gets worked on in the morning makes you 1% better at it than if you decided to sleep in. Over a year's time, you could be light years ahead in any skill that you apply yourself to during these morning hours. Waking up early gives a head start like no other, gaining a time advantage that is so personal and introspective.

In these early hours, the world pauses, free from the constant buzz of technology and the demands of daily life. It's a time for you to shine without distractions, to embrace the calm before the day's hustle begins. It's the perfect moment to unleash your creative energy and dive into any projects you've been putting off and unleash creative energy. If I waste any time in these early hours, it doesn't affect my day at all. Let's say I work at 9 am, but I am up at 6 am trying new things; I still start my 9 am day as usual except I got some extra hours of practice time in or reading or mindfulness. In the stillness of dawn, my mind can wander into the realms of creativity and reflection that the noise of the day often drowns out.

These hours are a great time for focused, undisturbed work, where productivity can truly flourish without the interruptions that come later in the day. For those who find the idea of early rising a challenge, it's worth considering what these quiet hours can offer. It's not just about pushing yourself to do more; it's about finding a space where you can be more— more thoughtful, more creative, more at peace. Rise early when you can, and discover the quiet strength that comes with greeting the dawn.

We are given this opportunity every day. So why not take advantage of it?

CHALLENGE #11: BECOME AN EARLY RISER

This challenge will help you transition to waking up early and create a morning routine that sets a positive, intentional tone for your day. The goal is to build consistency and make the most of those quiet, productive morning hours.

Step 1: Start Small

Day 1: The Hardest Day

- Set your alarm for 5:00 AM (or your desired early wake-up time).
- Even if you only get a few hours of sleep, get up when the alarm goes off. This is your reset day.
- Embrace the tiredness—it's your ticket to an earlier bedtime tonight.

Day 2: Build Momentum

- Go to bed by 9:00 PM (or earlier, depending on your wake-up time) to ensure you get a full 8 hours of sleep.
- Wake up at 5:00 AM again. You'll feel more rested and ready to start your day.

Step 2: Create Your Morning Routine

Wind Down the Night Before:

- Prepare for the next day by laying out your clothes, packing your bag, and writing a to-do list. This eliminates small tasks in the morning and lets you focus on your routine.

Morning Rituals (15–30 Minutes Each):

1. **Journaling:** Write down your thoughts, goals, and reflections. Use this time to set intentions for the day.
2. **Reading:** Read a few pages of a book that inspires or educates you.
3. **Meditation:** Spend a few minutes focusing on your breath and visualizing how you want your

day to unfold.

4. **Movement:** Do a 15-minute bodyweight workout, yoga, or stretching to wake up your body.

5. **Affirmations:** Speak or write positive affirmations to cultivate gratitude and self-love.

Keep It Simple: Start with one or two activities and gradually add more as your routine becomes a habit.

Step 3: Track Your Progress

Sleep Journal: Each morning, write down:

- What time you went to bed and woke up.
- How many hours of sleep you got.
- How rested you feel on a scale of 1 to 10.

Reflect on Your Routine: At the end of the week, journal on your experience:

- How did waking up early feel? Did you notice changes in your energy or productivity?
- What challenges did you face, and how can you overcome them?
- What's one small change you can make to improve your morning routine?

Step 4: Stay Consistent

- **Weekdays and Weekends:** Stick to your wake-up time every day, even on weekends. Consistency is key to making early rising a habit.
- **Adjust as Needed:** If you feel overly tired, adjust your bedtime slightly earlier to ensure you're getting enough rest.

Why This Matters

Waking up early gives you a head start on the day, offering quiet, uninterrupted time to focus on your goals and well-being. By building a consistent morning routine, you'll set a positive tone for the day and create space for growth, creativity, and self-care.

CHAPTER 12: THE ART OF SHOWING UP

"Most people don't even show up. Of the people who do, most don't really push themselves. So to show up and be disciplined about daily improvement. You are the rarest of the rare. "

—Ryan Holiday

Here on this strange planet, some Earthlings can't even manage to do the bare minimum and show up. It's like they are stuck in a strange paralysis: wake up, work, stare at screens, eat, sleep, repeat. Sometimes this cycle continues for decades. It's as if they've stepped out of a time machine and 20 years have passed, leaving them right where they started. This is a place you never want to be, but if you find yourself here, remember that it's not the end. Recognize that this moment is another one of those reset days, just like the sunrise. Each day, you get to decide how to spend your energy and waking hours.

The art of showing up isn't just about physically being somewhere; it's about consistently checking off those daily boxes on your calendar and reminding yourself of your incredible potential. You're transforming from a night owl to a morning person, from a casual drinker to a devoted journaler. You are a practitioner in the art of showing up, and by supporting yourself in mastering these daily habits, you've become an artist.

You are an artist, my friend.

Being present means more than just being physically there. It means truly engaging in the moment and whatever activities are right in front of your nose. Being where you say you will be, doing what you say you will do. Most people are on autopilot, daydreaming, lost in thoughts about the past or future, smiling and nodding just to get by. Truly showing up is a revolutionary act, and you are a revolutionary!

This guide is about keeping things simple, much like sticking to the fundamentals in sports. You need to nail the basics before moving on to more complex tasks. You've gotta nail that dribble before you hit the court. I mean, think about those basketball legends—they practically grew up with a ball in hand. You'd spot 'em dribbling their way to school and back, their obsession for the game shining through every bounce. Think about when you first learned to tie your shoes. At first, it felt like an intricate puzzle, but with time and practice, you became so proficient that you no longer needed to glance at your shoelaces. Well, that's the level of mastery we're aiming for when it comes to life's fundamentals.

These fundamentals should include good sleep, nutritious eating, reading, journaling, staying active, and practicing meditation. Master these basics, and you'll master life itself. Waking up each day, knowing you've checked off these essential tasks, sets you up for success. Few feelings compare to the satisfaction of engaging in a consistent daily routine in which you're prioritizing these fundamental tasks.

Imagine the future you, looking back on 365 days of unwavering commitment to daily habits, with stacks of journals filled with thoughts and affirmations. This future you thanks the present you for the dedication and support. You, in this moment, must become your biggest fan, whispering, "You can do it," and urging yourself to go the extra mile.

Mastering the art of showing up means committing to the fundamentals daily. It's about creating a routine that supports your growth and well-being, making sure you're mentally and physically ready to take on each day. It's about keeping your word and doing what you said you'd do. By showing up consistently, you're laying the foundation for a successful, fulfilling life. Remember, each small step you take today brings you closer to the future you desire.

BEING PRESENT MEANS MORE THAN JUST BEING PHYSICALLY THERE.

IT MEANS TRULY ENGAGING IN THE MOMENT... BEING WHERE YOU SAY YOU WILL BE, DOING WHAT YOU SAY YOU WILL DO.

CHALLENGE #12: BUILD YOUR ACCOUNTABILITY SYSTEM

This challenge will help you master the art of showing up by creating a personalized accountability system. The goal is to turn your intentions into consistent actions and ensure you stay on track with your goals.

Step 1: Define Your Goals

- **Choose 1–3 Daily Habits:** Pick habits that align with your priorities, such as waking up early, journaling, exercising, or meditating.

- **Set Clear Intentions:** Write down why these habits matter to you and how they'll help you grow.

Step 2: Choose Your Accountability Method

Pick one or more of the following strategies to hold yourself accountable:

Team Up for Success:

- Gather a small group of friends, family, or colleagues who are also working on self-improvement.

- Share your daily goals with the group and check in at the end of the day. Celebrate wins and reflect on what didn't get done—without judgment.

Bet on Yourself:

- Partner with a friend and set a financial stake. For example, if you don't complete your daily habit, you owe them $20 (or an amount that motivates you).

- Have them check in with you daily to ensure you're staying on track.

Hire a Coach or Mentor:

- If you're serious about leveling up, consider working with a coach or mentor who can provide guidance, support, and accountability.

Public Declarations:

- Share your goals publicly on social media, a blog, or with close friends. The act of declaring your intentions creates external pressure to follow through.

Track Your Progress:

- Use a journal, app, or calendar to track your daily habits. Mark each day you complete your goals and reflect on your progress at the end of the week.

Step 3: Reflect and Adjust

At the end of the week, journal on your experience:

- How did accountability help you stay consistent?

- What challenges did you face, and how can you overcome them?

- What's one small change you can make to improve your accountability system?

Why This Matters

Accountability transforms intention into action. By creating a system that works for you, you'll build the discipline and consistency needed to show up every day and achieve your goals. Remember, showing up is half the battle—accountability keeps you in the fight.

CHAPTER 13: THE POWER OF CONSISTENCY

"The greater danger for most of us isn't that our aim is too high and miss it, but that it is too low and we reach it."
—Michelangelo

We aliens might find it baffling, but Earthlings often struggle with consistency in their daily lives. Imagine a species capable of incredible technological advancements, yet they frequently fall into patterns of procrastination and inactivity. Many Earthlings spend countless hours staring at little screens, trapped in cycles of distraction. It's not uncommon for them to spend up to eight hours a day on these devices, often engaging in activities that offer little real benefit. Sometimes they dream year after year about becoming great artists but only pick up their paintbrushes for a few minutes a week. Or they hear an amazing symphony in their heads and go to their instruments, play a few notes, and then stop. Perhaps they're waiting for a better time to finish it? Who knows what these Earthlings are thinking? They seem to believe that a better, more perfect time is coming that will somehow offer the ideal conditions to finally begin their endeavors. However, we aliens know from experience that there's no better time to start than right now, and no better place to begin than right where you are. That's why we're here on earth—because we realize this vibrant, miraculous planet has everything we need to live a truly beautiful life.

I remember a time when I encountered a fundamental principle of success that forever changed my perspective. It was taught to me by a remarkable Earthling mentor, Brian Johnson of Heroic. He showed me the key to unlocking my potential—or as we might call it, my Power.

The formula he shared goes like this:

$$(ENERGY \times FOCUS \times GOALS)^{CONSISTENCY}$$

Let's break it down with an example. Suppose you're living a lifestyle that leaves you exhausted and mentally scattered. Your energy is at rock bottom—let's say, a 1 out of 100. Your focus, disrupted by bad sleep and lack of self-reflection, is also a 1. Goals? Hard to have any when you're in survival mode, so that's another 1. But here's a twist—you've been remarkably consistent in this pattern. So, let's score your consistency at 100. Applying Brian's formula: $1 \times 1 \times 1$ equals 1. Now, raise 1 to the power of 100. The result? Still 1. Your power, in this scenario, is minimal.

Now, imagine a different scenario. You've been firing on all cylinders—waking up early, journaling, reading, meditating, eating healthy, exercising. You're a powerhouse of energy, focus, and goal-driven action—all at a perfect 100. But, after just five days, you hit the brakes. A weekend of indulgence leads to a week of inactivity. Suddenly, your consistency drops to near zero. Despite the million in potential power, a consistency of 0 reduces it all back to 1. 100 x 100 x 100 = 1,000,000!!! 1,000,000 to the power of 0 is ... 1.

But don't lose hope. The beauty of this formula is its emphasis on consistency. Let's say you learn from this. You adapt, persist, and maintain your newfound habits. Your consistency climbs back to 100. Now, $100 \times 100 \times 100$ raised to the power of 100—it's an astronomical number, a metaphor for limitless potential. 100 x 100 x 100 ^ 100 = Infinity. Your power is literally infinite with consistency!

This, my fellow extraterrestrial friends, is the power of consistency on Earth. It's not about the intensity of your efforts in spurts; it's about steady, relentless pursuit. With unwavering consistency, your power isn't just substantial; it's boundless.

BUILDING CONSISTENCY INTO YOUR LIFE

Now, let's translate this concept into our daily habits and progress. The key is not to overwhelm yourself with grand, strenuous efforts right off the bat. Instead, the real power lies in your consistency—the regular, steady application of effort, no matter how small.

If there's a singular, pivotal lesson to embrace, it's the art of showing up, over and over again. It's about making a commitment to do something meaningful each day, however small it may seem. Imagine the transformation you could undergo in just 90 days. Think of the person you could become—a version of yourself that's stronger, more capable, more enlightened.

So, ask yourself: How badly do you want to change? How eager are you to step away from the life you've known and flourish into the best version of yourself? The journey to such transformation is less daunting than you might think. It starts with a single step, and this tiny first step becomes two, and then three, and then four—and once this small, consistent effort gets going, the momentum is unstoppable, propelling you forward in unimaginable ways.

Remember, the kindness and effort you extend to yourself today pave the way for a brighter, more fulfilled tomorrow. Your future self is a direct product of the choices and actions you take today. Be good to future you, and in turn, that future self will be the guardian of all your goals and dreams.

CHALLENGE #13: BUILD CONSISTENCY, ONE DAY AT A TIME

This challenge will help you master the art of consistency by focusing on small, daily actions that compound over time. The goal is to show up every day, no matter how small the effort, and build momentum toward your goals.

Step 1: Choose Your Daily Habits

Pick 1–3 Habits: Select habits that align with your priorities, such as journaling, morning movement, healthy eating, reading, or mindfulness.

Start Small: Commit to just 5–15 minutes per habit each day. For example:

- Journal for 5 minutes.
- Stretch or walk for 10 minutes.
- Read for 15 minutes.

Step 2: Create a Daily Ritual

Morning Routine: Start your day with one or two of your chosen habits. For example:

- Write in your journal to set intentions for the day.
- Do a short stretching routine or take a walk.

Evening Reflection: End your day by reflecting on your progress. Ask yourself:

- Did I show up for my habits today?
- What went well, and what can I improve tomorrow?

Step 3: Track Your Progress

Use a Habit Tracker: Keep a journal, calendar, or app to mark each day you complete your habits. Seeing your streak grow will motivate you to keep going.

Celebrate Small Wins: Acknowledge your progress, no matter how small. Every day you show up is a victory.

Step 4: Reflect and Adjust

At the end of the week, journal on your experience:

- How did it feel to show up consistently? Did you notice changes in your energy or mindset?

- What challenges did you face, and how can you overcome them?

- What's one small change you can make to improve your consistency next week?

Step 5: Level Up

Add a New Habit: Once you've mastered your initial habits, add one more to your routine.

Increase Time or Intensity: Gradually increase the time or intensity of your habits. For example, extend your reading time from 15 to 20 minutes or add a few more stretches to your routine.

Why This Matters

Consistency is the key to unlocking your potential. By showing up every day, even in small ways, you build momentum and create lasting change. Remember, it's not about perfection—it's about progress. Each day you show up, you're one step closer to becoming the best version of yourself.

CHAPTER 14: PURPOSE-DRIVEN BEINGS

"The purpose of life is not to be happy. It is to be useful, to be honorable, to be compassionate, to have it make some difference that you have lived and lived well."

—Ralph Waldo Emerson

Out of all the planets in our infinite universe, why choose Earth? The answer isn't about the planet itself—any good planet will do. It's about the purpose you bring to your life here. Earthlings are naturally driven by a need for purpose, yet many struggle to uncover what theirs truly is. Happiness and a sense of control often stem from having clear, daily goals. That's why mastering the discipline of setting meaningful goals is essential. Without them, humans risk succumbing to boredom—one of their greatest obstacles on the path to greatness.

When I first arrived on Earth, I felt lost and overwhelmed by the sheer volume of self-development information. Thousands of books, all seemingly recycling the same confusing and often contradictory advice. It wasn't until I shifted my focus toward discovering my own purpose that things began to click. This journey ultimately led me to write this book, with the goal of distilling the most essential truths in a way that was both easy to understand and apply.

Self-development became my purpose, and through it, I found a passion for helping others navigate their own paths. This book is my attempt to make the journey toward personal growth less daunting and more accessible. While there are countless self-help books out there, many lack a clear, cohesive message. My aim is to simplify these concepts and present them in a way inspires real change.

As you journey through life on Earth, it's essential to recognize that mental health and purpose are universal challenges. Just as beings across the cosmos face their own struggles, Earthlings also battle with maintaining a sense of purpose. Imagine a species that is capable of incredible advancements, yet often remains trapped in cycles of distraction and inactivity. Many dream of greatness but take minimal steps toward achieving it, waiting for perfect conditions that rarely come. This leads to stagnation and unfulfilled potential.

Purpose is like a guiding star in the vast universe of experience. It provides direction, motivation, and a sense of meaning. Without it, Earthlings can easily slip into spiritual and mental decline, feeling as though they are merely existing rather than truly living.

The evidence is clear: Having a sense of purpose is not just a philosophical concept but a practical necessity for both mental and physical well-being. Purpose fuels resilience and empowers individuals to live more fulfilling, productive lives. By setting meaningful goals and striving to achieve them, humans can significantly enhance their overall happiness and quality of life.

Viktor Frankl, a psychiatrist and Holocaust survivor, emphasized that finding meaning and purpose is critical for psychological health. His theory of logotherapy is based on the idea that the primary drive in humans is the search for meaning. Frankl demonstrated, even in the most unimaginable circumstances, that purpose could give people the strength to endure. His insights, born from extreme suffering in concentration camps, show that purpose is not a luxury but a necessity for survival and personal fulfillment.

Cultivating a daily habit of seeking challenges is essential. Challenges keep us engaged and prevent life from feeling aimless. Without purpose, people may fall into a state of spiritual shutdown or turn to destructive behaviors in an attempt to feel something or fill the void left by aimlessness. The most successful individuals on Earth are those with clear goals and a drive to pursue them consistently.

Research shows that people who pursue personally significant goals are generally happier. Happy people don't just have goals—they take consistent action toward achieving them. At some point, however, daily action can start to feel like a grind, and this is where professionals distinguish themselves from amateurs. They stick to their routines, even when boredom sets in.

For instance, it typically takes YouTubers about five years to reach one million followers. This achievement requires daily effort, research, development, and countless iterations. Rarely does someone fail after dedicating five years of consistent, focused work. The path to mastery is built on practice, and more often than not, the biggest threat to success is not failure but boredom. Every successful person has faced this challenge and learned to overcome it by falling in love with the process.

Having a sense of purpose is the cornerstone of a fulfilling, productive life. It provides the motivation and resilience needed to overcome life's inevitable challenges. By setting meaningful goals and working toward them consistently, humans can lead happier, more satisfying lives. Remember, every small step you take today brings you closer to the future you desire. Be kind to your future self by embracing purpose and consistency in your daily actions.

REMEMBER WITHOUT PURPOSE, PEOPLE FALL INTO A STATE OF SPIRITUAL SHUTDOWN OR TURN TO DESTRUCTIVE BEHAVIORS, THE **MOST SUCCESSFUL** ON EARTH ARE THOSE **WITH CLEAR GOALS AND A DRIVE TO PERSUE THEM.**

CHALLENGE #14: DISCOVER YOUR PURPOSE AND BUILD CONSISTENCY

This challenge will help you uncover your purpose, set meaningful goals, and take consistent action toward achieving them. The goal is to create a life filled with intention.

Step 1: Define Your Purpose

Reflect on What Matters: Spend 15–20 minutes journaling about your passions, values, and the impact you want to have on the world. Ask yourself:

- What brings me joy and fulfillment?
- What problems or causes do I care deeply about?
- How do I want to be remembered?

Write a Purpose Statement: Summarize your reflections into a single sentence that captures your purpose. For example:

- *"My purpose is to inspire others through creativity and kindness."*

Step 2: Set Meaningful Goals

Break It Down: Identify 1–3 long-term goals that align with your purpose. For example:

- Write a book.
- Start a community project.
- Learn a new skill.

Make Them SMART: Ensure your goals are Specific, Measurable, Achievable, Relevant, and Time-bound. For example:

- *"I will write 500 words of my book every day for the next 90 days."*

Step 3: Create a Daily Action Plan

Small, Consistent Steps: Break your goals into daily or weekly actions. For example:

- Write for 30 minutes each morning.

- Spend 1 hour each weekend planning your community project.
- Dedicate 15 minutes daily to learning a new skill.

Integrate into Your Routine: Attach these actions to existing habits (e.g., after breakfast, before bed) to make them easier to stick to.

Step 4: Track Your Progress

Use a Journal or App: Record your daily efforts and achievements. Reflect on:

- What did I accomplish today?
- What challenges did I face, and how can I overcome them?
- How did today's actions bring me closer to my purpose?

Celebrate Wins: Acknowledge your progress, no matter how small.

Step 5: Embrace the Process

Find Joy in the Journey: Focus on the daily actions rather than the end result. Ask yourself:

- What did I learn today?
- How did I grow or improve?
- What can I do tomorrow to stay motivated?

Overcome Boredom: When motivation wanes, remind yourself of your purpose and the impact your actions will have.

Step 6: Reflect and Adjust

At the end of the week, journal on your experience:

- How did it feel to take consistent action toward your goals?
- Did your purpose statement resonate with you, or does it need refining?
- What's one small change you can make to improve your consistency next week?

113

Why This Matters

A lot of these exercises may seem repetitive, but that's the point. The goal is to build consistency through daily actions until they become second nature—where you don't even have to think about them. Purpose gives your life direction, but it's consistency that turns dreams into reality. By showing up every day and putting in the work, you create momentum, build muscle memory, and step into a flow state where everything feels more natural.

Remember, the journey is just as important as the destination. Keep going!

CHAPTER 15: MAKE LIFE A GAME

" Comfort is a drug. Once you get used to it, it becomes addicting. Give a weak man consistent sex, good food, cheap entertainment and he'll throw his ambitions right out the window. The comfort zone is where dreams go to die "

—Earthling Proverb

One of the easiest traps Earthlings fall into is the appeal of cheap entertainment—video games, TV, endless scrolling on social media. It's a seductive but ultimately hollow distraction. So, my question for you: Did you travel all this way to earth to be a creator, or to be an NPC?

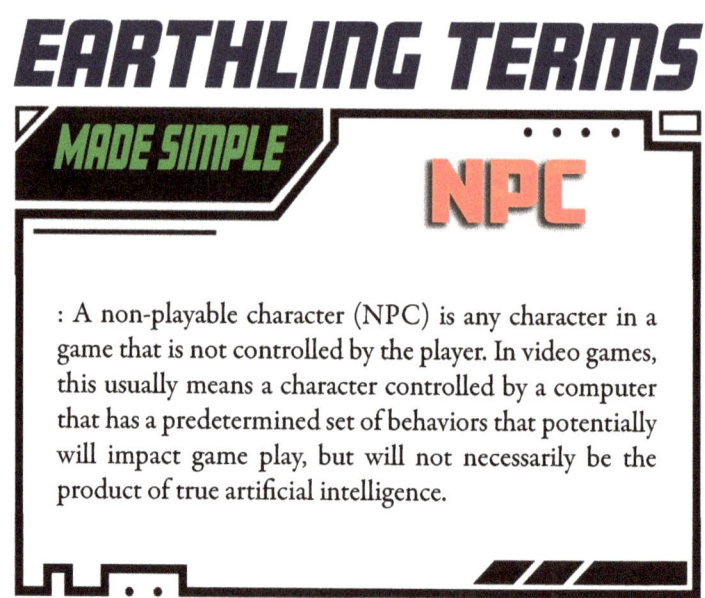

EARTHLING TERMS
MADE SIMPLE
NPC

: A non-playable character (NPC) is any character in a game that is not controlled by the player. In video games, this usually means a character controlled by a computer that has a predetermined set of behaviors that potentially will impact game play, but will not necessarily be the product of true artificial intelligence.

Consider this: It's alarmingly easy for the protagonist of your own story (AKA, you) to devolve into an NPC, living life on the side, disengaged from the main quest. What truly separates you from the background characters in games—those sipping drinks at the bar or sweeping streets endlessly? They're programmed for a monotonous loop: wake up, work, perform menial tasks, and repeat. It's a static existence, empty of growth or change.

Now, take a hard look at what your life could become here on earth if you're not careful. Do you, wise alien, really want to end up caught in a similar loop as so many of these poor earthlings? Waking up, working, eating, socializing, drinking, sleeping—rinse and repeat, day after day, year after year. How many people around you resemble these programmed characters, following the same routine they've had for decades? The old math teacher habitually grading papers at the end of the bar since 1989, or sweet Gail who's been a cashier at Walmart for as long as you can remember. These are lives lived in the background—the quintessential NPC's.

But is this the role you truly desire for your new life here on earth? I don't think so. Recall our discussion on habits. Habits are the architects of our identity; they shape our actions, which in turn define us. Breaking away from the NPC cycle starts with reshaping your habits.

Transform your perspective. Make yourself the protagonist of your own life story in this elaborate and unpredictable game called life. If you don't you might just become an NPC, living in the background of another character's journey.

Start viewing your life as a game—not in a superficial sense, but with the understanding that you have the agency to direct your journey, face challenges, grow, and achieve your goals. It's about embracing the adventure, the unpredictability, and the endless potential for personal growth and achievement.

Here are some ways to view life as a game:

1. **Main Quests:** Goals are essentially dreams that are written down. Life, when viewed as a series of these goals, becomes an engaging quest. Consider these your main quests. Document them and create a strategy for their accomplishment using a calendar. This method lends both clarity and purpose to your objectives, transforming abstract aspirations into achievable milestones.

2. **Leveling Up:** Each new skill or improvement you achieve is gaining a level. Every book you read, every day you maintain a consistent routine, every page you journal, every session of meditation, every workout, and every instance of self-reflection brings you closer to mastery.

3. **Boss Battles:** Significant challenges in life are your boss battles, and everything you've experienced has led up to these defining moments. They present unique opportunities to demonstrate your skills and strategies. Reflect on your preparedness for these challenges. Are you ready to confront them directly, or do you need time to devise a plan? Framing obstacles in this manner can transform them into manageable, even exhilarating experiences. This is the intersection of preparation and opportunity—this is your time to shine!

4. **Keeping Score:** Just as games provide scores and feedback, you can seek feedback in life to understand your progress. Constructive criticism and self-reflection are ways to 'check your score' and plan your next moves. There's no shame in asking your peers to weigh in on your performance and how you can improve—if anything, this is how you will level up faster than those who are too prideful or too "tough" to ask for advice.

5. **Adapting Strategies:** Success in games often hinges on adaptive strategies, and the same holds true for life. Embrace flexibility and be ready to adjust to new situations for both success and personal growth. It's

Do not let the shortcomings or negativity of others impact your poise or self esteem. The most effective way to counter naysayers is with positivity. Greet negativity with a smile and enjoy yourself. This is your best response. By staying aware of the situation and the motives of those around you, you put yourself one step ahead of any potential adversaries.

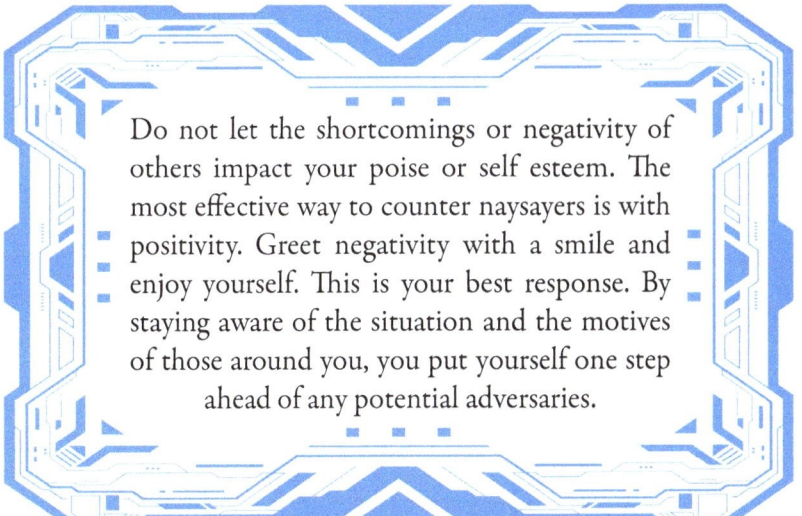

△ LOADING

○ Level up skills

important to stay vigilant of your surroundings and the dynamics of the people around you to maintain an edge.

6. **Pause Menus for Breaks:** Just as games have pause menus, life requires breaks. These are essential to avoid burnout and allow for reflection and recovery. Remember, recovery is as important as the action itself. Use downtime for sleep, meditation, and visualization to prepare for upcoming challenges.

7. **Replaying Levels:** In games, replaying levels is a normal part of the learning process. Similarly, in life, embracing failure as a learning opportunity is key. Repeated efforts build the 'muscle memory' needed for success. If you don't fail, you can't learn. If you don't put in your reps, how can you get faster and more efficient?

8. **Resource Management:** Effective management of resources like time, money, and energy is crucial in life. Consider what adjustments you can make to optimize these resources. Could altering your sleep schedule, perhaps going to bed earlier and waking up at 5 am, help you achieve more and get ahead of your schedule? Reflect on the aspects of your daily routine that you can rearrange to enhance your productivity and efficiency.

9. **Unlocking New Areas:** Maintain a sense of curiosity and be open to exploring new interests. Embrace a beginner's mindset and be willing to step out of your comfort zone. Whether it's enrolling in a new class or engaging in a different activity, you can unlock new passions and opportunities at any time. Even small changes, like choosing a different route for your walk, opting for stairs instead of an escalator, or cycling to work, can bring fresh perspectives into your life's journey. You have journeyed all this way in search of fresh experiences and are now finally doing it! Keep going, you can do it!

10. **Forming Alliances:** Building and maintaining posi-

tive relationships is vital for both personal and professional success. Collaborate with others; a strong team can achieve goals more effectively than a single overburdened individual.

When you view life as a game, you harness the power to own your own life. You transform mundane tasks into engaging challenges and goals. This shift in perspective not only makes daily routines more enjoyable but also empowers you to take control of your journey on Earth. Instead of drifting aimlessly or succumbing to the allure of passive entertainment, you become an active participant in your own story.

Remember, you have the agency to direct your journey, face challenges, grow, and achieve your goals. Embrace the adventure, the unpredictability, and the endless potential for personal growth and achievement. By turning your life into a series of quests, leveling up your skills, and tackling boss battles, you unlock new levels of fulfillment and success. Consistently check your progress, adapt your strategies, and never forget to take breaks when needed.

So, the next time you find yourself tempted to slip into NPC mode, remind yourself of the vibrant, dynamic game you have the power to play. Your life is an epic quest, and you are the hero. It's time to show up, take charge, and make every moment count.

CHALLENGE #15: A WORLD OF DREAMS AND ADVENTURES AWAITS

This challenge is designed to help you embrace life as an epic game, complete with quests, leveling up, and boss battles. Each quest will push you to explore, connect, and grow, transforming ordinary moments into extraordinary adventures. Ready to play?

Step 1: Choose Your Quests

Pick 3–5 quests from the list below to complete this week. Each quest is designed to help you level up in different areas of your life.

Quest List:

The Helping Hand Quest

- **Objective:** Help someone in need without expecting anything in return.
- **Example:** Assist a stranger with groceries, guide a lost pet home, or donate to a cause you care about.
- **Reward:** +10 Kindness Points (and the satisfaction of making someone's day brighter).

Forge a New Alliance

- **Objective:** Connect with someone new and build a meaningful relationship.
- **Example:** Strike up a conversation at a coffee shop, attend a networking event, or join a local club.
- **Reward:** +15 Charisma Points (and a potential new ally for your journey).

Decode Your Environment

- **Objective:** Explore and learn about the natural world around you.
- **Example:** Use the iNaturalist app to identify five plants or animals in your area.
- **Reward:** +10 Wisdom Points (and a deeper connection to your environment).

Unlock a New Zone

- **Objective:** Explore a place you've never been before.
- **Example:** Visit a new park, trail, or neighborhood. Spend at least an hour soaking in the sights and sounds.
- **Reward:** +10 Exploration Points (and a fresh perspective).

Restore the World

- **Objective:** Give back to your community through a small act of kindness.
- **Example:** Clean up trash, donate unused items, or leave encouraging notes for strangers.
- **Reward:** +15 Heroism Points (and the joy of making a positive impact).

Expand Your Skill Tree

- **Objective:** Learn a new skill or hobby.
- **Example:** Try a new recipe, learn a basic phrase in a foreign language, or practice a new yoga pose.
- **Reward:** +10 Skill Points (and a new tool for your personal toolkit).

Discover a Hidden Treasure

- **Objective:** Find something unique or inspiring in your local area.
- **Example:** Visit a quirky café, a hidden bookstore, or a serene park. Capture the moment with a photo or journal entry.
- **Reward:** +10 Luck Points (and a memorable experience to cherish).

Step 2: Track Your Progress

- **Create a Quest Log:** Use a journal, app, or notebook to track your quests, rewards, and reflections.
- **Celebrate Wins:** After completing each quest, take a moment to acknowledge your achievement and reflect on what you learned.

Step 3: Reflect and Level Up

At the end of the week, journal on your experience:

- Which quests did you enjoy the most, and why?
- How did these quests help you grow or see the world differently?
- What's one new quest you'd like to add to your life moving forward?

Why This Matters

Life is an epic game, and you're the hero of your own story. By embracing challenges, exploring new horizons, and connecting with others, you'll unlock new levels of fulfillment and growth. Remember, every quest you complete brings you closer to becoming the best version of yourself.

CHAPTER 16: UNCOMFORTABLY COMFORTABLE

"The most important conversation is the one you have with yourself."

—David Goggins

The comfort zone is the graveyard of dreams. If you don't work on finding comfort in discomfort, your chances of success on this planet are slim. The reality is straightforward: the only way to improve this skill is by deliberately placing yourself in uncomfortable situations on a regular basis. Start with small steps, such as turning off the air conditioning in your living space or drinking room-temperature water. Challenge your reliance on conveniences; try cooking your own meals and eliminate simple pleasures. Keep in mind that a seed must completely destroy itself in order to blossom into a flower.

When you envision the person you aspire to become in the next five years, you must recognize that achieving that vision requires dismantling parts of your current self. This process begins with the practice of stepping out of your comfort zone. There will inevitably be aspects of yourself that become unrecognizable to both you and those around you. So, what can you do every day that just scares the hell out of you? Can you commit to doing it consistently from this point forward?

Consider a practice that many Thriving Earthlings engage in: the Cold Plunge. Rarely will you hear someone say, "I love immersing myself in freezing cold water." Most people dread it and experience significant anxiety just at the thought of it. However, they do it anyway, not only for its documented health benefits but primarily for the purpose of pushing themselves to confront profound discomfort daily and gradually improve their ability to handle it.

When I initially started cold plunging, I could barely endure 30 seconds, and it felt as though my legs were going numb. However, with consistent effort, day by day, my tolerance grew —45 seconds turned into a minute, and now I routinely spend between 4 to 5 minutes in the cold plunge, sometimes even twice a day. I understand that not everyone has the resources to purchase a cold plunge, but there are affordable ways to create one at home using an aquarium chiller. If that's not an option, you can immerse yourself in a cold river or take cold showers until you gain access to one.

 Alternatively, you can start with a sauna, exposing yourself to the other end of the temperature spectrum, and aim to stay inside for 15 to 20 minutes. Identify that point of discomfort and make a conscious effort to remain just a bit longer each time. This practice can extend to your eating habits, such as delaying your first meal of the day or attempting a full fast, helping you become more accustomed to discomfort. There are countless ways to cultivate comfort with discomfort. By practicing this daily, you will empower yourself to conquer any challenge, as each time you push beyond your comfort zone, you gradually dismantle parts of your past self and level up.

CHALLENGE #16: BUILD RESILIENCE THROUGH DISCOMFORT

This challenge will help you embrace discomfort as a tool for growth. By deliberately placing yourself in uncomfortable situations, you'll build resilience, confidence, and the ability to thrive in adversity.

Step 1: Identify Your Fears

Journal Your Fears: Write down 3–5 things that scare you or make you uncomfortable. These could be physical, social, or emotional challenges. Examples:

- Cold plunges or cold showers.
- Public speaking or starting a conversation with a stranger.
- Fasting or delaying meals.
- Asking for a discount or negotiating.
- Trying a new skill or hobby that intimidates you.

Step 2: Take Action

Daily Discomfort: Commit to doing at least one uncomfortable thing every day. Start small and gradually increase the intensity. Here are some ideas:

1. Cold Exposure: Take a cold shower or immerse yourself in cold water for 30 seconds. Gradually increase the time as you build tolerance.
2. Social Courage: Strike up a conversation with a stranger or ask for a discount at a store.
3. Fasting: Delay your first meal of the day by an hour or two. Gradually extend the fasting window if comfortable.
4. Skill Challenge: Try something new that scares you, like singing in public, dancing, or learning a new language.
5. Physical Challenge: Do a workout that pushes your limits, like a high-intensity interval training (HIIT) session or a long hike.

Step 3: Document Your Progress

Keep a Discomfort Journal: Each day, write down:

- What uncomfortable thing you did.
- How you felt before, during, and after.
- What you learned from the experience.

Step 4: Reflect and Adjust

At the end of the week, journal on your experience:

- Which activities pushed you the most, and how did you feel afterward?
- What challenges did you face, and how can you overcome them?
- What's one new uncomfortable activity you'd like to try next week?

Step 5: Level Up

Increase the Intensity: Gradually make your challenges harder. For example:

- Extend your cold shower to 2 minutes.
- Fast for an extra hour.
- Speak in front of a larger audience.
- Celebrate Wins: Acknowledge your progress and reward yourself for stepping out of your comfort zone.

Why This Matters

Discomfort is the gateway to growth. By consistently pushing your boundaries, you'll build resilience, confidence, and the ability to thrive in challenging situations. Remember, the discomfort you face today is the strength you'll have tomorrow.

CHAPTER 17: CLOSED MOUTHS DON'T GET FED

"Luck is what happens when preparation meets opportunity"
—Seneca

Many Earthlings struggle to get what they want because they believe their goals are unattainable. The power of intentional asking, a vital element of manifestation, is often grossly underestimated. If you're not familiar with the concept of manifesting, here is the simplest way to think of it:

EARTHLING TERMS

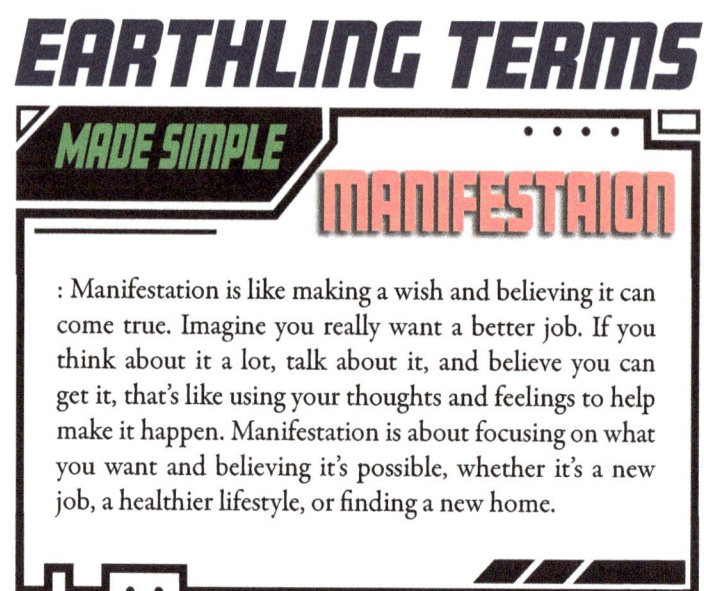

MADE SIMPLE

MANIFESTAION

: Manifestation is like making a wish and believing it can come true. Imagine you really want a better job. If you think about it a lot, talk about it, and believe you can get it, that's like using your thoughts and feelings to help make it happen. Manifestation is about focusing on what you want and believing it's possible, whether it's a new job, a healthier lifestyle, or finding a new home.

It's common on this planet to poke fun at those who seem to romanticize manifestation excessively—the young, 'witchy' types surrounded by crystals and plants, flooding social media with messages like, "Why aren't you in Bali? Just manifest it! Why are you still stuck in that day job?" While it's easy to view this as mere fanciful thinking, true manifestation is more substantive and requires hard work.

Effective manifestation relies on three critical elements: preparation, opportunity, and the buffer of time. It's not about instantaneously achieving grandiose dreams, like becoming the world's greatest guitar player overnight when you've only just begun to strum the strings. Realistic, incremental improvements are the foundations of genuine change.

Take, for instance, American singer-songwriter Sierra Ferrell. If you're active in the Earthling independent music scene, chances are you've come across her captivating performances. With her hauntingly beautiful voice, vintage aesthetic, and genre-blending sound—a mix of roots, country, bluegrass, and jazz—she might seem like an overnight success. But the reality is far more complex and inspiring.

Sierra's journey began in Charleston, West Virginia, where she grew up in a poor family. Music was her escape, and she taught herself to play the guitar and fiddle as a child. However, her path to success was anything but linear. In her early twenties, Sierra lived a nomadic lifestyle, traveling across the country in a van, hopping freight trains, and busking on the streets of New Orleans and other cities. These years were marked by hardship—she often slept in her van, faced the dangers of life on the road, and witnessed the harsh realities of addiction and overdose in the communities she encountered.

Despite her natural talent, Sierra was shy and struggled with self-doubt. It wasn't until she crossed paths with fellow musician Todd Snider that her career began to take shape. Snider recognized her potential and encouraged her to embrace her gift. This pivotal moment gave Sierra the confidence to step into the spotlight. She began performing solo, busking in public spaces, and collaborating with other musicians, honing her craft and building a loyal following.

Her big break came when she was discovered by Rounder Records, a legendary label known for its commitment to roots and Americana music. Sierra's debut album, "Long Time Coming," released in 2021, was a critical and commercial success. The album showcased her unique sound, blending old-timey influences with modern storytelling, and earned her widespread acclaim. But it was her sophomore album, "Trail of Flowers," released in 2024, that truly cemented her place in music history. The album swept the Grammy Awards, winning four trophies and beating out some of the biggest names in the industry. It was a complete sweep of the American roots category, a rare feat that underscored her artistry and the universal appeal of her music.

Sierra Ferrell's story is a testament to the power of perseverance, authenticity, and resilience. Her journey, far from overnight, exemplifies the saying, "Luck is what happens when preparation meets opportunity." She didn't just wait for her big break—she worked tirelessly, embraced discomfort, and stayed true to her unique voice, even when the road was uncertain.

What makes Sierra's story even more remarkable is her ability to transform adversity into art. Her music is deeply personal, often drawing from her experiences on the road and her struggles with self-doubt and hardship. Songs like "In Dreams" and "The Sea" resonate with listeners because they are raw, honest, and deeply human. Sierra's authenticity is her superpower, and it's what sets her apart in an industry often dominated by polished, formulaic acts.

Sierra Ferrell's rise is a reminder that success is rarely a straight line. It's a winding road filled with challenges, setbacks, and moments of doubt. But for those who are willing to embrace discomfort, stay true to themselves, and keep showing up, the rewards can be extraordinary. Sierra didn't just find success—she created it, one note, one song, and one performance at a time.

Now, interstellar traveler, let's focus on you. What small steps can you take today to positively shape your future self on this planet? Are you aiming for a job promotion, or perhaps yearning for a remote position to embrace the freedom of travel? If remote work is your target, a good starting point is to explore your existing network. Is there anyone you know who is already living this lifestyle? Reach out to them, inquire about their path, and learn from their experiences.

Remember, 'closed mouths don't get fed.' Realizing your aspirations requires venturing out of your comfort zone and actively pursuing your goals. Embracing change means undertaking new, sometimes uncomfortable tasks. This might mean reaching out to professionals you haven't met before or even boldly stepping into the office of a company you aspire to work for and asking to speak with someone who could help you secure a position. What's the worst that could happen? A 'no'? While rejection may close one door, it also provides the perspective to recognize other doors that are just waiting to be opened.

To build confidence in this approach, here's a practical exercise: The next time you order food, ask for a complimentary drink. When you buy a coffee, request an upgrade to a larger size. Whenever you make a purchase at a store, ask for a discount. Many people might not mind and simply accommodate your request, while others might do the very worst thing—say 'no.' Either way, each experience is a step towards becoming better at asserting yourself and pursuing what you want.

STOP THE SELF DOUBT,
YOU'RE MAGICAL.
LET GO OF EGO, BE SELFLESS.
REMEMBER YOUR STRENGTH.
LIFE IF BRIEF,
BUT WHEN IT'S GONE,
LOVE GOES ON AND ON.

CHALLENGE #17: THE ART OF BOLD ASKING

This challenge will help you strengthen your ability to ask for what you want—whether it's help, opportunities, or even small favors. Many people hesitate to ask because they fear rejection, but mastering the skill of asking can open doors you never imagined.

Step 1: Define What You Want

Start by identifying three to five things you truly want but have been hesitant to ask for. These could be professional, personal, or financial goals. Examples:

- A raise or promotion at work.
- A chance to work on an exciting project.
- Help from a mentor or industry expert.
- A collaboration with someone you admire.
- More support in your personal life (from friends, family, or a partner).

Step 2: Reframe Rejection

Shift your mindset—a "no" is not a failure. Instead, it's a step toward finding the right opportunity. Every successful person has faced rejection. The key is to keep asking.

Step 3: Make Three Asks

Challenge yourself to ask for three things that make you slightly uncomfortable. Some ideas:

- **At Work:** Ask for feedback, a meeting with a higher-up, or additional responsibilities.
- **In Your Network:** Request an introduction, a mentorship, or career advice.
- **In Everyday Life:** Ask for a discount, a free upgrade, or a special favor.

You may get a "yes," a "no," or a "maybe"—but you will always gain confidence.

Step 4: Strengthen Your Ask

Not all asks are created equal. To improve your chances of success:

- **Be clear and direct.** Avoid vague language. Say, "Would you be open to mentoring me once a month?" instead of "Can I pick your brain?"
- **Offer value.** If you're asking for a favor, consider what you can give in return.
- **Expect success.** People are more likely to say "yes" when you ask with confidence rather than hesitation.

Step 5: Reflect in Your Asking Journal

Each time you ask for something, write down:

- What you asked for and how you framed it.
- The response you received.
- How it felt to ask.
- What you learned from the experience.
- How you'll adjust your approach next time.

Why This Matters

Asking is a superpower. Those who dare to ask—even in the face of rejection—are the ones who create new opportunities, deepen connections, and move closer to their goals. This challenge isn't just about getting a "yes" but about building the muscle of boldness so you stop holding yourself back.

What will you ask for today?

CHAPTER 18: IN ORDER TO RECEIVE, YOU MUST GIVE

"The law of giving is very simple: If you want joy, give joy. If love is what you seek, offer love. If you crave material affluence, help others become prosperous."

—Depak Chopra

As a new arrival on Earth, you may have noticed a curious trend: Many Earthlings seem to hold on tightly to what they have, fearing its loss. But remember, fellow travelers, the art of thriving on this planet isn't just in accumulation but in the graceful dance of give and take. By understanding that giving and receiving are the lifeblood of our existence, we unlock the doors to abundance and fulfillment in ways we never imagined.

Let's move beyond the idea of actively pursuing your desires and dive into the art of ensuring that your endeavors bear fruit. In every interaction, there exists a delicate balance of give and take, for the exchange of energy is the heartbeat of the universe. When this natural flow is disrupted, we find ourselves out of sync with the world around us. To sustain the circulation of abundance, be it wealth or any other aspiration, we must actively engage in both giving and receiving. The word 'currency,' which we use to describe money, is derived from a Latin term meaning "to run or flow." Money is a representation of the life energy we expend and subsequently receive through the services we provide to others. Like a river, money thrives on constant movement; stagnation leads to decay. When we clutch onto wealth, focusing solely on possession rather than circulation, we obstruct its flow back into our lives.

The intentions behind our acts of giving and receiving are of paramount significance. Genuine, wholehearted giving without any expectation of return amplifies the energy behind the gesture. Conversely, giving grudgingly carries no such energy. If giving feels like a loss, then it isn't true giving and will not contribute to your growth. It's vital to understand that giving extends far beyond monetary transactions; it encompasses every aspect of our lives. If you seek love, become a beacon of love and share it with the world. If you desire friendship, radiate approachability and genuine friendliness. If you wish to be heard, first lend a compassionate ear to others. The more you give, the more you will receive. By embracing generosity in all its forms, you keep the abundance of the universe flowing into your life.

One practical way to put this principle into action is by offering a gift to everyone you encounter. And remember, these gifts need not always be monetary or material in nature. Simple gestures such as offering your undivided attention, expressing gratitude, dedicating your time to assist others, or merely listening with genuine care can be profoundly meaningful gifts. These acts cost nothing but possess the power to enrich both the giver and the receiver on a profound level.

As you journey through life here on earth, challenge yourselves to practice this art. Tomorrow, as you orbit around the sun, offer a gift, however small, to each being you encounter. Observe not just their reaction, but also how it transforms your own energy.

Ask yourselves, are you merely existing on this vibrant planet, or are you contributing to its vast, interconnected web of life? The universe, in its infinite wisdom, has brought you here not just to take but to give, to not just survive but to thrive. In the words of one of Earth's great poets, Oscar Wilde, 'To live is the rarest thing in the world. Most people exist, that is all.' Choose to live. Choose to give. And watch the universe conspire with you in ways you never imagined.

CHALLENGE #18: THE ART OF GIVING

This challenge will help you cultivate a spirit of generosity and experience the transformative power of giving. By practicing small acts of kindness and service, you'll create a ripple effect of positivity in your life and the lives of others.

Step 1: Choose Your Acts of Giving

Pick 3–5 acts of giving from the list below to complete this week. Each act is designed to help you connect with others, contribute to your community, and experience the joy of generosity.

Give to Someone in Need

- **Objective:** Offer financial or material support to someone who could use it.
- **Example:** Donate to a crowdfunding campaign, buy a meal for a homeless person, or contribute to a local charity.
- **Reflection:** How did it feel to give without expecting anything in return?

Share Your Skills

- **Objective:** Use your talents to help others.
- **Example:** Cook a meal for a neighbor, help a friend with a home project, or teach someone a new skill.
- **Reflection:** What skills do you have that can make a difference in someone's life?

Help the Earth

- **Objective:** Contribute to the well-being of the planet.
- **Example:** Pick up trash in your community, plant a tree, or organize a local clean-up event.
- **Reflection:** How does caring for the Earth make you feel more connected to the world around you?

Reach Out to the Lonely

- **Objective:** Offer human connection to someone who seems isolated.
- **Example:** Strike up a conversation with a stranger, call a friend who's been quiet lately, or write a heartfelt note to someone who needs encouragement.
- **Reflection:** How did your act of kindness impact the other person—and you?

Challenge Yourself to Give Daily

Set a personal goal to complete as many acts of giving as possible in one day. Aim to give 5–10 small gifts, such as compliments, smiles, or acts of service, in a single day.

Why This Matters

As you incorporate more giving into your life, you'll begin to notice a shift. You'll find that each act of generosity brings its own reward, not always in the form of something tangible, but in the sense of fulfillment and connection it creates. By embracing the spirit of giving, you open yourself up to a world of possibilities, where the energy you put out into the universe returns to you in the most unexpected and enriching ways. So, take on this challenge and watch how your life begins to transform, one generous moment at a time.

CHAPTER 19: MEDIA DEPRIVATION

"The quieter you become, the more you can hear."
—Ram Dass

One thing that you'll undoubtedly notice as you settle here on this planet is the Earthling's absurd habit of spending an inordinate amount of their daily lives distracted. It's nearly impossible to navigate a full day without some form of interruption, be it a catchy tune in a store, an advertisement on a video, or snippets of strangers' conversations. This ongoing stimulation is a hallmark of life on Earth. Yet, the real question is: How does this constant barrage of stimuli affect you? While many Earthlings might not consciously notice it, this relentless sensory input can subtly influence the subconscious. That's why the practice of media deprivation is essential.

Many Earthlings are so accustomed to constant media exposure that they hardly realize it. They distract themselves from reality, whether it's through listening to the radio in the car, wearing headphones at the gym, or playing background music or podcasts at home while doing chores. Each of these activities, though seemingly harmless, can numb the mind, preventing you from fully engaging with the present moment, as well as with your own thoughts.

A day devoid of external distractions is a rare and enlightening experience. In this quiet space, memories and unresolved emotions can surface. However, there's no need for alarm. This process allows unexpressed feelings to emerge, an essential step in your progress in the game of life. Think of it as completing a vital side quest, necessary for reaching higher levels of understanding and self-awareness.

CHALLENGE #19: HOW TO PRACTICE MEDIA DEPRIVATION

The journey of media deprivation is simpler than it appears: The key is to eliminate all distractions. This means no music, TV, reading, social media, or any form of entertainment. Naturally, essential tasks for work, such as checking emails or responding to messages, are allowed. However, be vigilant to avoid aimless scrolling or seeking frivolous distractions, like amusing yourself with spam emails. The essence of this exercise is to immerse yourself in solitude with your thoughts.

During this period, allow yourself only tools that foster creation. This includes:

- Pens and journals for writing or drawing
- Art supplies for painting or crafting
- Musical instruments for composing or playing
- Cameras for photography and video
- Microphones for recording

These are instruments of creation, not consumption.

Inner Circle Support

Before you begin, inform those close to you about your media deprivation endeavor. This ensures they understand your unavailability and know how to reach you in emergencies. It's crucial your inner circle is aware and supportive of your quest.

Do Not Disturb Mode

Switch your communication devices to silent mode for a period ranging from 24 to 72 hours, or even longer if you prefer. The length of this exercise is flexible, tailored to your comfort and needs. However, it's worth noting that many experience significant breakthroughs after the 48-hour mark.

Be mindful that it's common to inadvertently break the rules of media deprivation, which may lead to feelings of guilt or self-criticism, and the mistaken belief that you need to start over. Remember, such slip-ups are part of the process. Instead of dwelling on them, acknowledge the lapse and gently steer yourself back to the exercise. This approach helps in maintaining focus and commitment to your media deprivation journey without undue self-abuse or stress.

Boredom, Mindfulness, and Unloading Mental Clutter

Boredom will inevitably make an appearance during this exercise. When it does, welcome it as a vital part of the process. Find a comfortable spot to lie down and gently shift into a meditative state. If you notice your mind wandering or latching onto specific thoughts, don't fight these moments. Instead, embrace them as opportunities. When a thought persists, signaling its significance, take that as your cue to write it down. Jot these thoughts down succinctly, just enough to jog your memory later. The goal is to acknowledge these thoughts briefly and then guide yourself back to a state of meditation with minimal delay.

Your primary objective is to transfer all your thoughts onto paper, effectively decluttering your mind. Think of your brain as a computer with limited storage capacity. Writing down your thoughts acts as a way to clear mental clutter, similar to how one might clear junk mail or empty the trash bin on a computer. This practice helps create space for new, potentially more constructive thoughts.

During your media deprivation journey, it's normal for past memories to bubble up to the surface. It could be a persistent song, a disagreement from your childhood, or a cringe-worthy moment from your teenage years. Whatever form they take, document these memories. These periods of reduced external stimuli provide a unique opportunity to explore and connect the dots between these resurfacing memories. Delving into them can reveal patterns and underlying themes, offering insights into your subconscious mind.

Documenting Lapses

If you find yourself breaking the deprivation, jot it down. Detail how it happened and why. This introspection offers insights to your behavior and thought processes. Whether you inadvertently clicked on a link or found yourself watching commercials in a waiting room, understanding these moments is crucial.

Why This Matters

Practicing media deprivation isn't just about finding silence; it's about tuning into the inner voice that guides your actions and thoughts. It's a powerful tool for breaking free from the monotonous routine, propelling you from the role of an NPC to that of the Main Character in the grand narrative of your life.

CHAPTER 20: UNDERSTANDING MENTAL ILLNESS

"A way to get somewhere you've never been is to go somewhere you've never gone before"

—Dalai Lama

As we continue our journey on this planet, it's essential to recognize that mental illness is not a uniquely Earthling phenomenon. Just like physical ailments, struggles with mental health are something that beings across the known universe experience. This understanding can help us approach these challenges with empathy and support, letting Earthlings know they're not alone in their battles.

Mental illness manifests as an internal storm, where thoughts are clouded by sadness, anxiety, or confusion, even when there's no apparent reason. It's a relentless tempest raging within, making it difficult for individuals to carry out everyday tasks or find joy in activities they once loved. This storm can be incredibly isolating, but it's crucial to remember that support and understanding can make a significant difference.

In every interaction, we have the opportunity to be a beacon of calm in someone's turbulent mental landscape. By acknowledging the universality of these struggles, we can foster a sense of unity and compassion. Together, we can create an environment where seeking help is seen as a strength and where mental health is given the same importance as physical health.

THE CONNECTION BETWEEN MENTAL HEALTH AND METABOLISM

The Earthling brain, a remarkable organ, consumes a significant chunk of the body's energy—around 30%, to be precise. It's the command center for thoughts and emotions, but like any other part of the body, it can get sick too. When mental illness strikes, it affects the way people think, feel, and behave. But here's a twist: The energy used for thinking, feeling, and maintaining mental well-being is closely connected to how the body processes energy—a function known as metabolism.

Think about it. If about one-third of our metabolism fuels our thoughts, isn't it logical that thinking can make us tired? Have you ever noticed how it's challenging to think clearly when you're hungry or exhausted? Or how stimulants like caffeine and sugar can give your brain a boost? These connections might seem strange at first, but they make sense once you dig into the science behind them.

A revolutionary new understanding developed by Harvard psychiatrist Dr. Chris Palmer for the first time unites our existing knowledge about mental illness within a single framework: All mental disorders are metabolic disorders of the brain. Palmer challenges the traditional approach to diagnosing and treating mental disorders. He introduces a metabolic perspective, suggesting that the root causes of mental health issues, including anxiety, depression, and post-traumatic stress disorders, might be closely linked to how our bodies process energy. It's a thought-provoking concept that could revolutionize the way we view mental health.

One intriguing idea that Palmer explores is the relationship between effective mental health therapies and the brain's metabolic demands. Strengthening metabolism to meet these demands might enhance or expedite these therapies. For instance, he could investigate how metabolic interventions complement other treatments, potentially making them more effective.

Palmer's book Brain Energy challenges established norms and offers valuable insights into the intersection of metabolism and mental well-being. If you're searching for a fresh perspective on mental health, exploring the metabolic lens might just provide the key to unlocking new possibilities for a healthier mind.

THE IMPORTANCE OF SEEKING HELP

It's crucial to remember that mental illness isn't anyone's fault, just like catching a cold isn't your fault. It can happen to anyone at any time, and the good news is, it's treatable. Just like when you're sick, you can go to doctors. A therapist is someone who specializes in helping with mental health, and they can give you the right kind of support to help make things better. Additionally, opening up to friends and family about what you're going through can provide a much-needed support system. Mental illness doesn't define a person, and with the right assistance, they can still lead a fulfilling life.

YOUR ROLE IN A WORLD GRAPPLING WITH MENTAL HEALTH ISSUES

We exist in a world grappling with a growing mental health crisis, where the prevalence of mental illnesses is on the rise. The purpose of this chapter is to heighten your awareness of the people around you. Your time on this planet is limited, and although you may be eager to make a positive impact, the decision to change ultimately rests with the individual.

Stay true to yourself, continue your personal growth journey, and remember that not all aspects of life hold the same significance. Take your well-being seriously, seek out like-minded individuals who understand your journey, and bear in mind that being part of a supportive community can be an incredibly motivating force. Nothing sustains motivation better than belonging to a tribe that supports and uplifts each other.

CHALLENGE #20: CULTIVATE MENTAL HEALTH AWARENESS

This challenge will help you deepen your understanding of mental health, support those around you, and prioritize your own well-being. By taking small, intentional steps, you'll contribute to a culture of empathy, acceptance, and care.

Step 1: Educate Yourself

Spend time researching different types of mental illnesses, their symptoms, and how they affect individuals.

Example: Read articles, watch documentaries, listen to podcasts or explore resources from organizations like the National Alliance on Mental Illness (NAMI) or Mental Health America.

Step 2: Listen Without Judgment

If someone shares their struggles with you, listen with empathy and without judgment. Avoid offering unsolicited advice—sometimes, being heard is enough.

Example: Use phrases like, "I'm here for you," or "Thank you for sharing that with me."

Step 3: Offer Support

If someone is struggling, gently suggest seeking professional support. Offer to help them find resources or accompany them to appointments if they're comfortable.

Example: Share information about local therapists, hotlines, or support groups.

Step 4: Practice Self-Care

Engage in activities that bring you joy, relaxation, and peace.

Example: Meditate, journal, take a nature walk, or spend time with loved ones.

Seek Help if Needed: If you're struggling, don't hesitate to reach out to a therapist or counselor.

Step 5: Use Your Voice

Share information about mental health to help break the stigma.

Example: Post on social media, share resources, or participate in mental health awareness campaigns.

Step 6: Reflect and Expand

At the end of the week, journal on your experience:

1. Which actions felt the most meaningful, and why?
2. How did this challenge change your perspective on mental health?
3. What's one new way you'd like to support mental health awareness moving forward?

Step 7: Deepen Your Impact

Gradually expand your efforts to support mental health. For example:

1. Volunteer with a mental health organization.
2. Organize a mental health awareness event in your community.
3. Advocate for mental health resources in your workplace or school.

Inspire Others: Share your experiences and encourage others to join the movement for mental health awareness.

Why This Matters

Mental health is a universal concern, and your actions can make a profound difference. By fostering empathy, offering support, and prioritizing your own well-being, you contribute to a world where mental health is understood, accepted, and cared for. Remember, the journey to mental wellness is a shared one, and your efforts can be a guiding light for others.

CHAPTER 21: WE ARE...

"If you want to go fast, go alone. If you want to go far, go together."

—African Proverb

If you were persistent enough to travel all the way to Earth, perhaps it's not surprising that you, curious traveler, are committed. For instance, by reading this book, you are committing yourself to taking the the first steps towards self-development. You are stepping out of the rat race and away from social norms to build the life you want. By being your biggest fan, staying positive and turning your dreams into reality. If you've made it this far, it's clear that your commitment to personal growth is unwavering, and you stand on the brink of extraordinary achievements.

I extend my heartfelt appreciation for your dedication and warmly invite you to join our community, should you feel inspired to do so. If this book has resonated with you, consider connecting with others who share your passion for growth and self-improvement. No matter where your journey began, we welcome all who have embraced the wisdom within these pages.

This book is intended to spark the transformation from passively observing life to actively thriving as a vibrant, engaged Earthling.

Now, I urge you to take a moment to add us to your network, wherever you may find us under the name "Stoic Rockstar." We've made it easy for you to connect with a community of creators and warriors who are hungry to carve their own path. One of the most powerful steps you can take is to immerse yourself in a culture where you no longer feel like an outsider. Transforming your life becomes far more attainable when you witness others already living it.

If you surround yourself with individuals who embody the habits you aspire to, you'll naturally adopt those habits yourself. Your culture sets the standard for what is considered normal, so why not surround yourself with people whose habits align with your aspirations? Each new connection is an opportunity to find common ground, and this book serves as the perfect icebreaker to spark those conversations. By transforming personal questions into shared ones, your daily habits become part of your identity, making this new way of life a lasting transformation.

CHALLENGE #21: HOW TO FIND YOUR TRIBE

The name of the game is community, and many Earthlings have completely lost touch with this after leaving grade school, which was the closest thing to community that some Earthlings may ever experience. Usually, after grade school, if Earthlings don't develop skills that involve community, they end up finding their tribe at bars, where they end up building a dependence on alcohol and late nights filled with bad foods and habits in a toxic environment. Now, here are some guaranteed ways to find community in healthy environments:

1. Join a Gym: Find a local gym built by locals. These gyms build communities that support each other with group workouts, hikes, and workshops. This is the best way to give yourself a reason to wake up early.

2. Pick Up a Martial Art: Martial arts with levels of competition are another great way to find a community, especially popular disciplines like Jiu-Jitsu. These martial arts show you the power of showing up and commitment, revealing how drilling and practicing fundamentals can develop into monumental gains of confidence.

3. Join a League: Was sports a big part of your life at one point? Almost every city has local leagues for people of all skill levels, from beginner to advanced, and in every sport imaginable, including soccer, golf, basketball, darts, archery, rock climbing, etc. The easiest way to find one is to do a quick internet search with the sport you are looking for and the city. For example, "Austin Texas Darts" will likely yield results.

4. Open Mic: Do you have a drive to perform and be creative? Drop by a local open mic and check out the local talent. Most open mics allow a mix of music, comedy, and poetry. Sometimes all it takes is seeing beginners perform to give you the confidence to try it out. That's how I started: Seeing that the people on stage were not rock stars, just normal people like me, performing on a Monday night with the single goal of gaining experience to hopefully play a bigger stage in the near future.

5. Join a Book Club: Having a hard time diving deep into

a book? Sometimes a book club is a great way to discuss and debate topics with a group of like-minded people.

Why This Matters

The most important part is never being afraid to be a beginner and just showing up. Every single person that ends up at one of these communities, even the ones who run it or are the most skilled, showed up just like you on day one and were probably just as nervous. It takes time, but if you find enjoyment in one of these activities or communities, they will dramatically impact your life in ways you cannot achieve alone or in isolation.

CHAPTER 22: BE GOOD TO FUTURE YOU

"The graveyard is the richest place on earth, because it is here
that you will find all the hopes and dreams that were never
fulfilled, the books that were never written, the songs that
were never sung, the inventions that were never shared, the
cures that were never discovered, all because someone was
too afraid to take that first step, keep with the problem, or
determined to carry out their dream."

—Les Brown

Interstellar travelers, you made it to the end! Let's wrap this up with
a lesson about time-travel. While you're probably well-aware of it,
did you know that the most basic and essential kind of time travel
involves how you treat yourself?

The final and most crucial lesson in this book is to be kind to your future self. Speak kindly to your present self and learn the art of forgiving your past self. You have a finite number of years on this planet before your earthly vessel begins to show signs of wear and tear, ultimately requiring you to navigate life with certain limitations. It's a choice between having challenges now and a smoother journey later, or an easier path now that may lead to greater difficulties down the road. The decision is entirely yours, and there is no shame in the path you choose.

Earth is home to a diverse array of individuals. Some, like David Goggins—renowned endurance athlete and former Navy SEAL—push the boundaries of what the human body can achieve, dedicating themselves to reaching the pinnacle of physical performance. Others simply desire a vessel that functions consistently well throughout their time on this planet. The choice is a deeply personal one.

It's important to remember that the journey of self-improvement should never be a path of self-aggression. The self-help movement, while immensely beneficial, can sometimes unintentionally imply that who you are right now is not enough, that you are somehow broken. This notion is harmful. Improving yourself should be about evolving into the best version of yourself while appreciating and loving who you are at each stage of your journey.

You are not broken. You are not incomplete. The desire to grow and improve should stem from a place of self-love and self-appreciation. Understand that the process of self-improvement is an act of kindness towards your future self, but it must be balanced with kindness towards your present self.

Self-compassion involves treating yourself with the same kindness, care, and understanding that you would offer to a good friend. Research shows that self-compassion is linked to numerous benefits, including lower levels of anxiety and depression, better emotional resilience, and even improved physical health.

When you are kind to yourself, you create a supportive internal environment that fosters growth and change. This doesn't mean you ignore your mistakes or avoid taking responsibility. It just means you recognize that being imperfect, failing, and experiencing difficulties are part of the shared human experience.

It's crucial to strike a balance between challenging yourself and accepting yourself. Pushing your limits and striving for improvement are vital, but so is acknowledging your current achievements and being content with who you are. This balance ensures that you don't burn out or become overly critical of yourself.

PRACTICAL STEPS TO BE GOOD TO FUTURE YOU

1. **Set Realistic Goals:** Aim high, but set achievable milestones to avoid becoming overwhelmed. Celebrate each small victory along the way.
2. **Prioritize Health:** Make choices that benefit both your current and your long-term physical and mental health. Regular exercise, balanced nutrition, and sufficient sleep are fundamental.
3. **Practice Mindfulness:** Stay present and engaged with your current experiences. This helps reduce stress and increase your enjoyment of life.
4. **Develop a Growth Mindset:** Embrace challenges as opportunities to learn rather than threats to your self-worth.
5. **Forgive Yourself:** Let go of past mistakes and learn from them. Self-forgiveness is essential for moving forward without carrying unnecessary burdens.

CHALLENGE #22: THE TIME TRAVELER'S PROMISE

This final challenge is designed to help you integrate the lessons of this book into your daily life by embracing self-compassion, honoring your journey, and committing to a future of growth and kindness. Let's close this cosmic adventure with a pledge to your past, present, and future selves.

Step 1: Write a Letter to Your Future Self

Objective: Reflect on your journey so far and set intentions for the person you want to become.

Action: Write a heartfelt letter to your future self 1 year from now. Include:

1. What you've learned about yourself during your time on Earth.
2. Goals you want to achieve (personal, professional, or spiritual).
3. A promise to treat yourself with kindness, no matter where life takes you.

Seal It: Store the letter in an envelope and mark the date to open it one year from today.

Step 2: The Daily Self-Compassion Ritual

Morning Affirmation: Start each day by looking in the mirror and saying:

"I am enough. I choose to grow with kindness today."

Evening Reflection: End each day by journaling:

1. One thing you did well today.
2. One small step you took toward your future self's goals.

Step 3: The Forgiveness Ceremony

Objective: Release past regrets and embrace self-forgiveness.

Action: Light a candle (real or symbolic) and write down one regret or mistake from your past. Read it aloud, then say:

> *"I release this burden. I forgive myself and choose growth."*

Destroy It: Safely burn or tear up the paper as a symbolic act of letting go.

Step 4: Future-You Day

Objective: Dedicate one day a week to choices that benefit your future self.

Examples:

1. Meal prep healthy food for the week.
2. Schedule a group workout class or mindfulness session.
3. Invest time in a skill or hobby that aligns with your long-term goals.
4. Take yourself on a creative date to experience something new.

Reflect: How did prioritizing your future self make you feel?

Step 5: The Gratitude Time Capsule

Objective: Celebrate your present self and the progress you've made.

Action: Create a "time capsule" with:

1. A list of 3 things you love about yourself right now.
2. A photo or memento that represents your current journey.
3. A note of gratitude to your past self for bringing you this far.

Bury It: Store it in a special place to revisit when you need a reminder of your worth.

Step 6: Reflect and Celebrate

At the end of the month, **journal on your experience:**

1. How has practicing self-compassion shifted your mindset?
2. What surprised you about writing to your future self?
3. What's one promise you'll carry forward beyond this challenge?

Why This Matters

Your journey on Earth is a delicate balance of growth and grace. By treating yourself with kindness—honoring your past, nurturing your present, and investing in your future—you become the author of a life rich in purpose and peace. Remember, self-compassion isn't a destination; it's the fuel for your journey.

FINAL WORDS

As you close this book, remember:
You are not just a traveler passing through Earth—
you are its co-creator. The choices you make today
ripple across time, shaping the legacy you leave
for your future self and the universe itself. Carry
these lessons like stardust in your pockets, and may
your journey be guided by curiosity, courage, and
boundless self-love.

GO FORTH, TIME TRAVELER. YOUR FUTURE IS WAITING.

CONCLUSION

Dearest interstellar traveler, you've reached the final pages of this guide—a toolkit designed to help you navigate the complexities and quirks of human life on Earth. With every chapter, you've gathered insights, strategies, and secrets that will allow you to blend in and thrive among Earthlings. But the work doesn't end here. This playbook is just the beginning.

Your future on this planet is unwritten, waiting for you to shape it with intention, adaptability, and courage. Remember, Earth is a dynamic stage, and the most successful players are those who not only master the rules but also know when to break them. Don't simply observe human society—participate in it. Lead it. Transform it.

Each choice you make, each connection you foster, ripples outward, influencing not just your journey but also the environment and lives around you. Harness that power wisely. Keep your focus clear, your humor sharp, and your ambitions boundless.

As you venture forth, carry this truth with you: the most rewarding outcomes don't come to those who merely survive—they come to those who dare to thrive. You've chosen to take that daring step, and that alone sets you apart.

Farewell, fellow traveler. May your time on Earth be prosperous, fulfilling, and just the right amount of unpredictable.

Books That Changed My Life

1. *Real Artists Don't Starve,* by Jeff Goins
2. *Atomic Habits,* by James Clear
3. *Discipline Is Destiny,* by Ryan Holiday
4. *Arete,* by Brian Johnson
5. *The Artist's Way,* by Julia Cameron
6. *The 48 Laws of Power,* by Robert Greene
7. *The Alchemist,* by Paulo Coelho
8. *Why We Sleep,* by Matthew Walker
9. *Brain Energy,* by Christopher Palmer
10. *The Power of Now,* by Eckhart Tolle
11. *Can't Hurt Me,* by David Goggins
12. *Man's Search for Meaning,* Viktor Frankle

About the Author

John P. Rosales

I create because I have to. If I stop, I do not just stop creating. I break. Obsession is my oxygen. I would rather be haunted by unfinished songs and impossible ideas than crushed by silence. Art is where I leave the pain, the disappointment, the failure, the rage. It is where I lose myself and find myself again. Cracked but still standing. It is not a hobby. It is how I survive. It is my therapy. My faith. It is why I wake up and why I dream. I do not need an audience to justify it. I listen. I feel it. I live it. Humans are creators. We need purpose like lungs need air. Viktor Frankl said it best. Those who have a why can bear almost any how. So I found my why. I make things. Even when it is messy. Even when no one cares. I do it to stay alive.

Stoic Rockstar is my world. I built it from nothing. I make music with Holy Death Trio. I write scripts. I direct films. I interview artists. I live on curiosity and movement. I believe in making art not content. I believe you find yourself through creation and you lose yourself when you stop. I do not apologize for who I am or who I am becoming. I try things. I fail. I improve. I keep going.

The Earthlings Playbook is everything I learned on the road. It is for the misfits, the outsiders, the quiet thinkers, the ones who have ideas boiling in their chest but no manual on how to get them out. If you want permission to become who you know you are deep down, take it. Create something real. Leave proof you were here.

JOURNAL HERE

www.ingramcontent.com/pod-product-compliance
Lightning Source LLC
Chambersburg PA
CBHW051310120626
46547CB00015B/2169